The English Garden

The English Garden

LAURENCE FLEMING
and
ALAN GORE

LONDON
MICHAEL JOSEPH

TO
ROBERTO BURLE MARX
AND
LUIS BARRAGAN

First published in Great Britain by
MICHAEL JOSEPH Ltd
27 Wrights Lane
Kensington, London W8
NOVEMBER 1979
SECOND IMPRESSION MARCH 1980

First published in Mermaid Books edition
SEPTEMBER 1982
SECOND IMPRESSION APRIL 1986

ISBN 0 7181 1816 2

Printed and bound in Hungary

Contents

Authors' Acknowledgments

First of all, the authors would like to thank the owners of all the gardens visited while making the television series and writing this book, and Mr. Richard Mervyn, director of the series, for his patience and interest.

For their generous help in many different ways, they would especially like to thank: The Duchess of Beaufort and the Duke of Beaufort, the Earl and Countess of Scarbrough, Lord and Lady Ridley, Lord and Lady Burnham, Lord and Lady Egremont, the late Sir Richard Cotterell and Lady Cotterell, and Sir Rupert Speir; Mrs. Elizabeth Atchison, Mr. and Mrs. Oliver Colthurst, Mr. William Crossman, Miss Charlene Garry, Mr. St. John Gore, Mr. John Harris and Miss Ann Hills, Dr. W. O. Hassall, Mr. E. M. Mitchell, Mrs. David Peake, Mr. Peter Reynolds, the President and Council of the Royal Horticultural Society, Mr. Peter Stageman and Dr. Brent Elliott, Dr. David Stuart, Mr. H. Stafford, Mr. Gerald Sunderland, Mr. Reginald Thompson and Miss Sarah Hann, Mr. Francis Valentine and Mrs. David Verey.

And, for her constant encouragement and amazing faith, Miss Diana Potter of Thames Television.

For her translations from the Latin on pages 11, 12 and 13, Susan Greig; for their skill and ingenuity in designing the book, Jeanette Graham and Phil Kay; for permission to quote from Clare Williams' translation of Thomas Platter, Messrs. Jonathan Cape; and for permission to quote from Gertrude Jekyll's *Colour in the Flower Garden*, Messrs. Newnes-Butterworths.

Programme Credits

Authors	Alan Gore and Laurence Fleming
Narration	Sir John Gielgud
Commentary	Alan Gore and Tony Bastable
Production Assistant	Sally Barnsley
Film Editor	Rosemary MacLoughlin
Graphic Designer	Bernard Allum
Director	Richard Mervyn
Producer	Diana Potter

List of Colour Illustrations

Sources for the black and white illustrations

The illustrations in this book are reproduced by kind permission of the following (numbers refer to page numbers):

John Bartholomew & Son Ltd: 215
John Bethell: 99, 239 (middle)
The Bodleian Library: 9
The British Museum: 19, 21
Country Life: 19, 21, 30, 31, 46, 54, 56 (top), 57 (top), 58, 60, 67–9, 71, 73, 76–7, 80, 82, 84–86, 88–91, 98, 101–105, 107, 109 (right), 110–117, 119–122, 124–126, 128–9, 138 (bottom), 139–40, 142–43, 145, 152, 154–6, 158, 165–6, 169, 173–6, 179, 181, 183–4, 186–194, 202–204, 208–213, 216–222, 225–30, 233
The Earl of Scarbrough: 10
The Holkham Library: 97, 147, 153
The Linnæan Society: 240 (bottom)
The National Portrait Gallery: 238 (top), 239 (bottom), 241 (top), 244 (bottom)
The National Trust: 32, 51, 109 (left), 137, 138 (top), 150–51, 232
Mervyn Pickwoad: 22
The *Radio Times* Hulton Picture Library: 148
Royal Academy of Arts: 240 (middle)
The Stroud Museum: 178
Gerald Sunderland: 10, 17, 18, 23–25, 27–29, 33, 35, 37–39, 41–43, 45, 47, 49, 51, 56–57 (bottom), 64–66, 72, 74, 81, 87, 94, 97, 131, 133, 135, 146, 147, 153, 172, 177, 178, 180, 182, 197, 214, 237, 238 (bottom), 240 (top)
The Vancouver Art gallery: 237 (top)

PART ONE

A Tapestry of Herbs and Roses,
to 1660

(Roundels)
Mediaeval garden implements for scything, digging and weeding. Only the scythe is still in use in the same form. *From a 13th century English manuscript*

A marble fountain—possibly imported from Italy by Lord Lumley for the garden at
Nonsuch Palace in Surrey—one of the earliest examples of an elaborate garden
ornament. *About 1580*

The Mists of Time

The soil in England has been cultivated for a very long time. It is now thought that man, in this country, has been a farmer, as opposed to a hunter, since 4000 BC.

One reason for this is that our native foodstuffs all very nearly approach the inedible. Not a single native cereal can be made even into a meagre porridge; the native fruit, the sloe, the elderberry, the damson, the crab apple, can hardly be eaten raw. Therefore, when emmer, an early wheat, came to the country from Western Asia six thousand years ago, our ancestors had to make it grow. Succeeding, they looked for other foreign crops.

They were Celts, a tribal race which spread across Central Europe north of the Alps, from the Black Sea to Denmark and Ireland and Scotland. Their great stone monuments were huge circles, their burial mounds circular at the base. They lived in round houses in round enclosures. In Europe, at least, their houses were colour-washed and painted in graceful, curving designs. Their jewellery and metal work made brilliant use of the asymmetrical, their decorations were sometimes very close to the abstract. Their priesthood, the Druids, moved freely throughout the Celtic world. Their religion included the worship of the spirits of groves and springs, trees and fountains.

Barley was brought here about three thousand years ago; spelt and eincorn, two other kinds of wheat, a little later, and oats about a hundred years before the birth of Christ. Rye came in the first century AD, and with these corn seeds, all of which were native to Asia, came the seeds of the scarlet poppy, the blue cornflower, the corn cockle and the corn marigold.

For vegetables, they grew a kind of broad bean, smaller than ours and with a brighter flower; beet, both red and white; the native carrot, which was white, and a purple one, native to Afghanistan; and the parsnip. They grew flax, buckwheat, the opium poppy and the native culinary herbs, chives, sweet cicely (myrrh), comfrey, tansy, marjoram, vervain (verbena) and basil (calamint). Hops and thyme, being native, were probably also grown; and one foreign crop which they certainly grew was woad.

An early impression of our ancestors was recorded by a friend of Quintus Cicero, a Roman politician, in a letter to him: 'If I were you, I certainly shouldn't buy slaves from Britain. They are incredibly stupid

Blue Patterns and Black Hands

Woad, *Isatis tinctoria*, is a handsome member of the family *Cruciferae*, to which the cabbage and the wallflower also belong, and is native to the Mediterranean. It is a greedy biennial. In England, in the Middle Ages, a law had to be passed prohibiting its growth on the same soil for more than three years. It was the principal source of blue dye until supplanted by Indigo, *Indigofera tinctoria*, native to the East Indies, towards the end of the seventeenth century. There was a woad industry in Suffolk until 1908.

The leaves of the first-year plant were cut with a scythe, washed and dried quickly in the sun. They were then ground into a smooth paste and made into heaps. A black crust formed, any cracks in it were sealed, and it was left covered for a fortnight. The crust was then mixed in and the whole was formed into solid balls. These were beaten to a coarse powder on the floor with wooden mallets, once more made into heaps and kept moist for twelve days, to induce fermentation. Thick fumes were produced, and the heaps were continually stirred with a shovel. It was then made into a heap for the dyer. Woad workers always had black hands.

The problem is to fix the dye, and it is thought that the ancient Britons may have used their own urine—cheap, plentiful and readily obtainable wherever it was required—for this purpose.

A simpler method was to infuse young woad leaves in hot water, add wood ash, and then to wash in the liquid. This turned the body blue. By using an excess of quicklime, a green dye could be produced.

By using a small quantity of lime water, and drying the resulting precipitate, a very strong blue dye was made. If this was mixed with oil or grease, it could be painted in patterns on the body. The Greeks are thought to have fermented the leaves in lime and water to make a blue-black dye. The leaves fermented in urine made a bright blue dye. The raw juice of the leaves turns the human skin black.

and quite incapable of learning. They really don't belong in any decent household.'

Other Roman writers noted their appearance. The poet Ovid, who died in AD 23, said they were green; the elder Pliny, a generation later, noticed that the women were 'the colour of the Ethiopians'. Herodian wrote: 'They mark their bodies with various figures of all kinds of animals, which is the reason they wear no clothes, for fear of hiding these figures.'

Julius Caesar first visited Britain in 55 BC. 'Nobody', he wrote later, 'would be silly enough to go there except to trade . . . The people inland do not grow corn—they live on meat and milk and dress in skins. All the Britons paint themselves with woad which gives them a dark-blue colour and makes them more frightening in battle . . . There is an enormous population, buildings very like those in Gaul all over the place, and big herds of cattle . . . There are trees of all the same varieties as there are in Gaul, but there are no beeches or pines . . . The climate is milder than in Gaul.'

The Romans were able to settle in southern Britain during the first century AD. The two nations seem to have remained separate. The poet Horace refers to 'the Britons, more remote than anyone else in the world' and 'the Britons, who are so *very* unpleasant to strangers'.

According to the historian Tacitus: 'The sky is foul with incessant rain and clouds, but there are really no sharp frosts . . . The soil is fertile and bears crops—except for olives and vines and all the other things that grow in warmer countries. They germinate late but shoot up quickly and the reason for both these phenomena is the same—the terrific dampness of both the land and the air. Britain produces gold and silver and other metals, making her well worth conquering.'

But the principal reason must have been that England was already the green and pleasant land that William Blake wrote about nearly two thousand years later.

The garden at the Flavian Palace—at what is now Fishbourne, near Chichester—was begun about AD 75. The Roman garden, in general, was a long rectangle joined to the house by a terrace, and this was sometimes shaded by a pergola over which climbing plants could be trained.

The gardens were enclosed by hedges, perhaps left open at the end if there were a view. In the towns, landscapes were painted on the wall at the end of the garden instead. The Roman hedges were of laurel, the Italian cypress (*Cupressus sempervirens*) or box, possibly myrtle. Box is native to England, but they could have brought over the others; or the native holly or yew could have been used instead.

At Fishbourne, down the centre of the rectangle, there was a path with a hedge on either side which went into alcoves at regular intervals, alternately rectangular and semi-circular. In these there were probably box bushes clipped into animal shapes; in Italy, they are more likely to have been busts, or statues. The Roman garden was carefully controlled. The lines were straight, the angles were right-angles and the curves were sections of a circle.

The Romans left Britain, unregretted, before AD 450. They left behind them the cultivated apple, the vine, the black mulberry and the fig, the sweet chestnut, the common walnut and the medlar. They probably introduced fennel, coriander, the nettle, pennyroyal, rue, borage, caraway and cumin, leeks, onions, garlic, globe artichokes, the cabbage in several forms, the turnip, the cucumber, asparagus, radishes, lentils, peas and celery.

Christianity came to England at the end of the sixth century; monasteries and convents were founded all over the country. In them horticulture, as opposed to agriculture, was possible—peace is one of the principal requirements of the garden. Further Celtic invaders, the Angles, the Saxons and Jutes, settled, bringing with them hemp for the making of rope and clothes, and cultivating the native flax to make linen. They seem to have lived in villages, to have shared their plough oxen and to have used the same kind of water-mill as the Romans.

They kept cattle and sheep, pigs in the forests, and bees. They used the scythe, a Celtic implement, and probably also the hook or sickle, which the Romans had used; and they stored their hay in ricks and mows, where it was less likely to go mouldy than in the closed lofts of the Romans.

A very important Herbal was produced in the tenth century, written in Anglo-Saxon, the language of the country at the time. At one time in the care of Glastonbury Abbey, it was translated into English in 1864, by the Reverend Oswald Cockayne.

'For fruits we know they had sweet apples, which are not indigenous to this country, pears, peaches, medlars, plums and cherries.' He mentions that they knew about grafting—the cultivated plum on to the native sloe, the pear on to the native *Pyrus domestica*—tells us that the cherry came originally from Turkey, that the peach is called 'the Persian apple' in the Herbal and that dates are mentioned in it.

Of the Herbal itself, he says that about a quarter of it seems to be translated directly from the Greek. Some plants, certainly, are referred to only by their Greek names, but a great many have Saxon ones. Sometimes 'the Engle' had a different name for a plant, and where this is the case it is probable that it was growing in England, either wild or in 'wort beds', which we may assume to have been beds of culinary or medicinal herbs. 'Worts' we would now call 'herbaceous plants', either annual or perennial. No instructions are given for their cultivation. They exist, and can be found.

'The Leechdom, or medecine book' is thought to have been written between AD 960 and 980 and we may assume that all the plants mentioned in it were available, either from the herb, or the culinary, garden. Some of

From the Glastonbury Herbal *written early in the tenth century:*

Feltwort [which we would now call mullein] is produced on sandy places and on mixens [middens].

This wort, which is named *senecio*, and by another name groundsel, is produced on roofs and about walls.

[Rosemary, here given its Greek name] by another name bothen, is produced on sandy lands and on wort beds.

Field more, or Parsnep, is produced on sandy places and on hills.

Dock is produced in sandy places, and on old mixens.

This wort, which is called raven's leek [orchis], is produced on high downs and in hard places, and also in meadows, and in cultivated lands, and in sandy ones.

Gentian is produced on downs.

Slite, sowbread [a cyclamen] is produced in cultivated places and on downlands.

Great wort [autumn crocus] is produced about hedges and in foul places.

Feverfuge or lesser curmel is produced on solid lands and on strong ones.

Strawberry is produced in secret places and in clean ones, and also on downs.

Yalluc [comfrey] is produced on moors and on fields, and also on meadows.

Lacterida [caper spurge] is produced in wet places and on shores.

Wherwet [cucumber], is produced nigh the sea and in hot places.

Orpine is produced on downs, and it is also sometimes planted on a wall.

Centimorbia [creeping Jenny] is produced in cultivated places, and in stony ones, and on downs, and in winsome places.

Sea holly is produced on fields and in stubborn places.

Electre, that is lupins, is produced against hedges and in sandy places.

From the Glastonbury Leechdom *between AD 960 and 980:*

Against lice: pound in ale oak rind and a little wormwood, give to the lousy one to drink.

Against mickle cold: take nettles, seethe them in oil, smear and rub all thine body therewith; the cold will depart away.

Give the sufferer from hiccups rue with wine, or nitre in sweetened wine, or carrot, or cumin, or ginger, or calamintha, or Keltic valerian.

For sore of the maw [stomach] take this same wort [comfrey], and mingle with honey and vinegar; thou shalt perceive much advantage.

For hip bone ache [sciatica], take some portion of a root of this ilk wort [peony], and with a linen cloth bind it to the sore; it healeth.

This wort [hop] is to that degree laudable that men mix it with their usual drinks.

For bite of snake, take leaves of this wort [woad], which the Greeks name *Isatis*; pound it in water, lay it to the wound; it benefits and removes the sore.

For wounds, though they be very old, take this wort [groundsel]; pound it with old lard, lay it to the wounds; it healeth them soon. [This also cured gout. As a poultice with salt, it relieved lumbago.]

For tooth ache, take a root of this wort [rosemary], give it to eat, without delay it removes the sore of the teeth; and let him hold the ooze in his mouth; soon it healeth the teeth.

For heartache [heartburn], take leaves of this same wort [bramble], pounded by themselves; lay them over the left teat; the sore passes off.

For the disease which is called lethargy, and in our language is denominated forgetfulness, take this same wort rue, washed in vinegar, souse then the forehead therewith.

For soreness and looseness of teeth, take this same wort [spearwort, elecampane], give it to eat fasting; it steadieth the teeth.

If a man's feet in a journey swell, take then waybread the wort [plantain], pound in vinegar, bathe the feet therewith; they soon dwindle.

This wort [watercress] is not sown, but is produced of itself in wylls [springs] and in brooks; in case that a man's hair fall off, take juice of this wort which one nameth *nasturtium*, and by another name cress; put it on the nose; the hair shall wax.

If anyone eateth the fruit of this wort [cucumber], fasting, it cometh to mischief to him, therefore, let everyone withold himself so that he eat it not fasting.

Against leprosy, take this same wort [latherwort, crowsoap, *Saponaria officinalis*], and meal, and vinegar, pound together; apply to the leper, he will be cured.

It [flower de luce, *Iris germanica*] also, moreover, is of benefit for sore of the head mixed with vinegar and ooze of the rose.

the proposed remedies seem to have been rather more agreeable than others.

'For hardness of the maw [stomach ache], take blossoms of this same wort [wood violet], mingled with honey, and soaked in very good wine; the hardness of the maw will be relieved.'

'For sore of the breasts, take this wort *Cannabis silvatica*, pounded with grease, lay it to the breasts; it removes the swelling; and if any gathering be there, it purges it away.'

'For sore of the eyes, that is what we call blearedness, take the ooze of this wort, which the Greeks name Mekon, and the Romans *Papaver album*, and the Engle call white poppy, or the stalk, with the fruit, lay it to the eyes.'

But the concern was not only with people.

'If sheep be ailing. Take a little new ale, and pour it into the mouth of each sheep; and manage to make them swallow it quickish; that will prove of benefit to them.'

The native Tulip.

2 The Honeysuckle.

3 The Oxlip.

The Buttercup.

5 The Yellow Flag.

6 The Mallow.

Native flowers. From *Flora Londinensis*, edition of 1835.

7 Blackberry.

8 Henbane.

9 Agrimony.

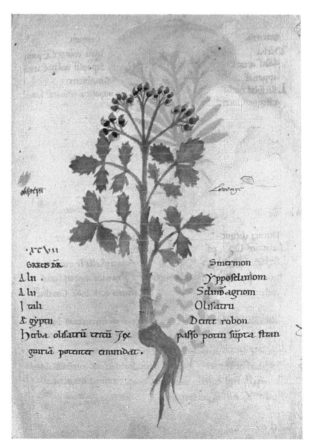

10 Alexanders.

From a herbal made in the Abbey of Bury St. Edmunds, late 11th century.

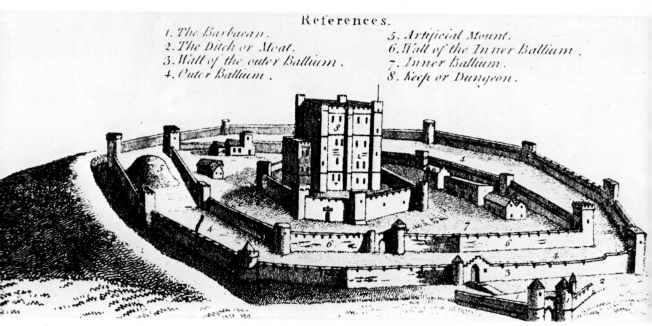

References.

1. The Barbacan.
2. The Ditch or Moat.
3. Wall of the outer Ballium.
4. Outer Ballium.
5. Artificial Mount.
6. Wall of the Inner Ballium.
7. Inner Ballium.
8. Keep or Dungeon.

A Successful Takeover

Norman castle, showing an early example of the Mount. At this date, the Mount would have been used for military purposes.

The Normans were originally Northmen from Denmark, and their conquest of England took place in 1066. One of their first contributions, both to horticulture and to agriculture, was to introduce the rabbit. Twenty years later, a great survey of England was made, called the Domesday Book, and it is interesting to find that forty vineyards are mentioned in it.

Gardening could only have been carried on within the castle or the monastery at this time, as civil war was frequent. The cloister gardens were, in general, in the form of a cross, that is to say a square cut into four squares by intersecting paths. At the centre, there would have been a statue, Christ Crucified, The Virgin Mary, or the patronal saint of the house, presiding over a spring or fountain.

The beds containing the plants were usually raised above the level of the ground, retained by a plank on edge. Medicinal herbs—the only hospitals were in the monasteries—and culinary herbs continued to be grown separately.

Where flowers were grown for their own sake, it is probable that they would have had some religious significance. In illustrated works of the time, mainly French or Flemish, there are references to Mary Gardens, which all contained roses and the Madonna lily, traditionally brought back by the Crusaders.

Not until the reign of Henry III do we find a description of a garden. On the 20 June 1250 it was decided to 'make two good high walls around

17

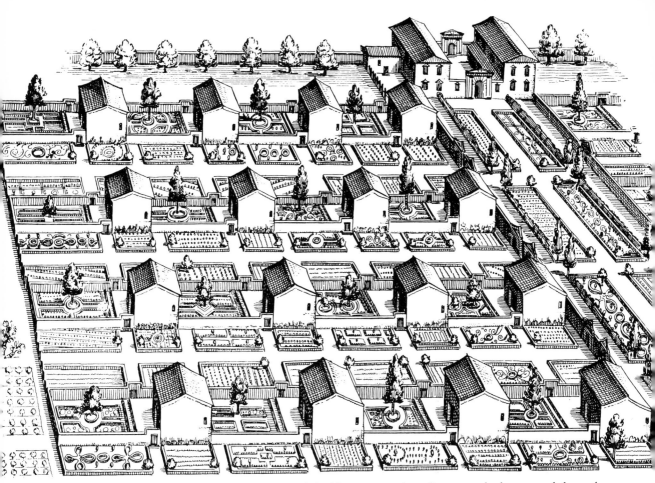

A monastery in Turin for hermits. Each monk had his own garden adjacent to the house, and the paths between their private gardens were planted with communal beds of herbs and vegetables.

the garden of the queen so that no one may be able to enter, with a becoming and pleasant herbary near the king's fishpond in which the same queen may be able to amuse herself . . . and with a gate from the herbary . . . into the aforesaid garden.'

The herbary was probably a herb garden, rather than the 'herber' or 'arbour' still referred to in the sixteenth century. The walls would most probably have been of stone 'mortered togither', though brick was also used. Mud walls were made by 'manie of the baser and poorer sort' and there were fences of 'bigge Canes set upright, by small poles held togither'. There is also a reference to hedges 'as thicke as a castel wall'.

The enclosed gardens seem, in general, to have been round. Grass was their basis and it has remained the foundation of the English Garden. There were grass walks and turf seats; bowling greens were in use as early as the thirteenth century. The wall, fence or hedge was usually at the top of a sloping bank of grass, in the Celtic way; and beyond them lay the 'flowery medes', grass meadows full of flowers.

18

A medieval garden, showing a turf seat enclosed by a simple form of trellis for supporting roses and other plants.

The colours of our native flowers are all very gentle, white, cream and unstrident yellows. The cowslip, the buttercup and the greater celandine are among our brightest yellows. The pinks are pure and pale, as in the dog rose and the honeysuckle, or else are bluish, like the ragged robin, rest harrow and the Cheddar pink. There is only one red, the scarlet pimpernel, a very soft colour; and the blues, the harebell, the speedwell and the field scabious, are rarely darker than an English sky. The purples are few and never fierce—the greater knapweed, the foxglove and the dog violet; and there is not a single orange. It is perhaps these colours that are best suited to the English light.

Not until 1440 do we find anything like a Gardening Book. *The Feate of Gardening* by Mayster John Gardener was written in verse at about that time. He devotes a whole section to the cutting and setting of vines; he writes 'Of Settyng and Reryng of Treys; of Graffyng of Treys; Of Settyng and Sowyng of Sedes; of Sowyng and Settyng of Wurtys; Of the kind of Perselye; Of other maner Herbs; Of the kind of Saferowne.'

He recommends staking with forks from the ash tree; that seedlings should be transplanted at the age of four weeks; that parsley should be sown in March and never allowed to grow high, when it will become 'blest and wanchy', thin and sickly. All herbs should be planted out in April and saffron—a profitable crop—planted only in 'beddys y-made wel with dyng'. He suggests grafting pears upon hawthorns and says:

Ye rynde of ye graffe and ye stok of ye tre
Most a-corde how that hit ever be.

and:

Cley mote be leyde to keep ye rayne owte.

Some of our native trees (there are about 50 in all)

Common Oak—*Quercus robur*	Least Willow—*Salix herbacea*
Sessile Oak—*Quercus petraea*	Large-leaved Lime—*Tilia platyphyllos*
Birch—*Betula pubescens*	Small-leaved Lime—*Tilia cordata*
Silver Birch—*Betula pendula*	Their hybrid, *Tilia europea*
A hybrid Birch—*pubescens x pendula*	Beech—*Fagus sylvatica*
Wych Elm—*Ulmus glabra*	Hornbeam—*Carpinus betulus*
English Elm—*Ulmus procera*	Alder—*Alnus glutinosa*
Smooth-leaved Elm—*Ulmus carpinifolia*	Hazel—*Corylus avellana*
Aspen—*Populus tremula*	Hedge Maple—*Acer campestre*
Black Poplar—*Populus nigra*	Mountain Ash—*Sorbus aucuparia*
White Willow—*Salix alba*	Service Tree—*Sorbus domestica*
Crack Willow—*Salix fragilis*	Whitebeam—*Sorbus aria*
Common Osier—*Salix viminalis*	Hawthorn—*Crataegus monogyna*
Goat Willow—*Salix caprea*	Ash—*Fraxinus excelsior*
Sallow Willow—*Salix cinerea*	Evergreens:
Eared Willow—*Salix aurita*	Yew—*Taxus baccata*
Tea-leaved Willow—*Salix phylicifolia*	Holly—*Ilex aquifolium*
Creeping Willow—*Salix repens*	Scots Pine—*Pinus sylvestris*
Downy Willow—*Salix lapponum*	Box Tree—*Buxus sempervirens*
Woolly Willow—*Salix lanata*	Juniper—*Juniperus communis*

For the setting of vines, he says this must only be done when the wind is in the west and that the vine 'schall have knottys tre', three joints giving three shoots.

Entrance to a trellised arbour providing support for climbing plants and therefore a shaded walk. *Late 15th century*

The Knot, the Maze and the Mount

The White Rose of York was probably *Rosa alba maxima* and the Red Rose of Lancaster *Rosa gallica maxima*. The bush on which both red and white roses traditionally grew was probably *Rosa damascena versicolor*, which has pink and white striped flowers, some much pinker, or whiter, than others. These roses had come to England from the Mediterranean and the Middle East, and the Civil Wars fought in their name ended in 1485.

Houses, as opposed to castles, could now be built. Gardens, or at least orchards, could be made outside the building, though possibly still within a moat.

The knot gardens, labyrinths and mazes which became a feature of the earliest English gardens, may have had their origins in the penitential mazes of the Christian Church. These were laid out in stone or tiles inside the church and the penitent performed the journey on his knees, saying particular prayers at particular points. Transferred outside, laid out in turf and gravel, they were at once a handsome decoration and a way of taking a lot of exercise in a small space. The maze at Wing, then in Rutland, and the labyrinth at Alkborough, then in Lincolnshire, are both round. Knot gardens were square.

Turf mazes are believed to have had some religious significance. This one is at Wing, formerly in Rutland.

22

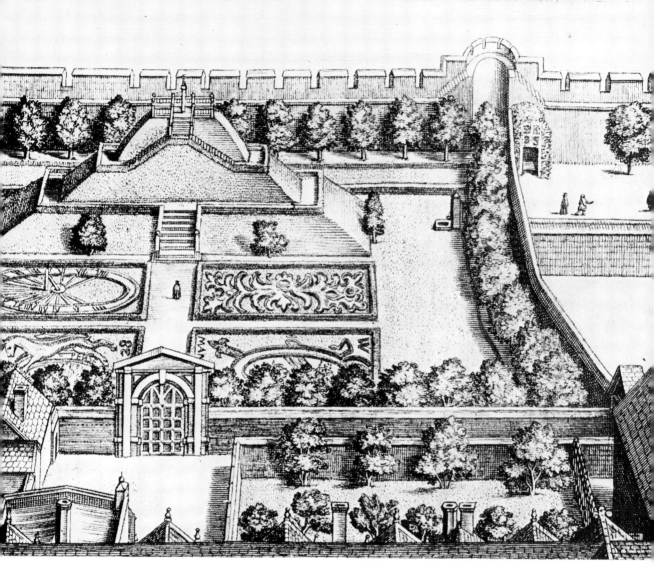

There is a story that a certain Duke of Buckingham, beheaded in 1520, invented an ingenious knot which could hang two men at the same time. This double knot can still be seen on a corbel at Thornbury, in Gloucestershire. Laid out four times within a square it made an interesting pattern.

The knots were made in combinations of hyssop, thyme, dwarf pinks, gillyflowers (border pinks), thrift, germander (*Teucrium chamaedrys*), rosemary, lavender, winter savory, lavender cotton and marjoram. Their clippings, as they had to be cut frequently, were scattered on the rushes on the floors inside, to combat the 'pestilent ayres'.

In the courtyard gardens, there was sometimes a wooden gallery with plants growing up it, a development perhaps of the Roman and the

New College, Oxford. The Mount is connected to a raised walk. *Early 17th century engraving*

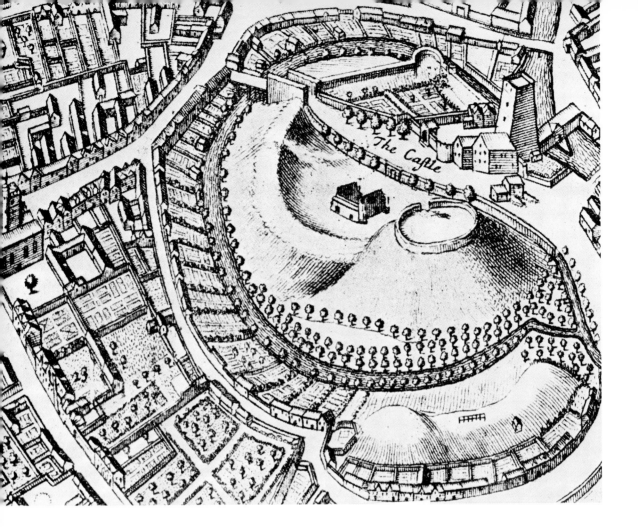

The Castle

mediaeval pergola. The mount, also, had sometimes been a feature of the mediaeval walled garden—Wadham and New College at Oxford both had one. Where it was not practical to make it of earth, it was made of timber and brightly painted. In shape, it was not unlike a Celtic burial mound.

Now it was moved outside the walled garden. In 1533 one was made at Hampton Court, overlooking the Thames. It had a brick foundation, and a path which wound up it 'like the turnings of cockle shells'. On top was a building of three storeys with windows on all sides, called The Great Round Arbour, the Lantern Arbour or simply the South Arbour. The mediaeval arbour had been made of clipped bushes; 'and shapen was this herber, roofe and all, as a prety parlour'. The Mount at Hampton Court was planted with 'quicksets', probably hawthorn bushes clipped low. There were flower beds with green and white rails—green for eternity, white for purity, the colours of the Welsh leek; there were bushes of juniper, yew, cypress, bay and holly and there were four hundred roses.

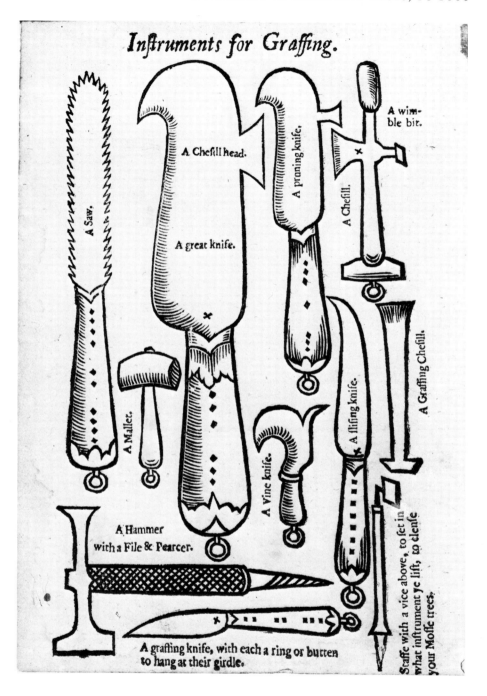

Instruments for grafting, from Leonard Mascall's *Art of Planting and Grafting*, 1572

The apricot was introduced at this time and the pippin—so called because it grew from a pip and did not need grafting—was 'fetched out of France' by the King's gardener. Plants looted from the newly dissolved monasteries also found their way into secular gardens.

Tools included knives 'to shred the quicksets', wooden and iron rakes, hatchets, chisels, grafting saws, cutting knives and cutting hooks.

In 1557, a new gardening book was published. It was called *Hundreth Good Pointes of Husbandrie*, by Thomas Tusser. It was more for the farmer than the gardener, but he advised, for instance, before cutting the lawn:

> No stick nor no stone leave unpicked up clene:
> for hurting thy sieth, or for harming thy green.

His advice is given month by month: 'Set gardeine beanes after Saint Edmond the King'. [November 16th]. He advises planting fruit trees at Christmas, 'while twelve tide doe last'.

> Set one from another, full twenty fote square:
> the better and greater, they yerely will bare.

> In Feverall rest not for taking thine ease:
> get into the grounde with thy beanes and thy peas.

> In March and in Aprille from morning to night:
> In sowing and setting good huswives delight.

In the mediaeval garden, the herb and flower gardens had been the province of the women and this seems to have continued into Tudor times, the vegetable garden then being included. Weeding was done only by women well into the eighteenth century.

> For flax and for hemp, for to have of her owne:
> the wife must in May take good hede it be sowne.

> In June get the wedehoke, thy knife and the glove:
> and wede out such wede, as the corne doth not love.

Tobacco from North America, spinach and the carnation from Europe—brought in by Protestant refugees—the potato from South America, all arrived about this time; and in 1571 appeared the first comprehensive guide to English gardening, with illustrations and plans for knots. *The Gardener's Labyrinth* was written by Thomas Hill, under the name of

Watering the garden with a pump in a tub. From Thomas Hill's *The Gardener's Labyrinth*, edition of 1586.

Didymus Mountain. Some of his advice is presented as having a Greek or Latin source, but much of it must have been the fruit of his own experience.

Garden plottes ought to be placed, farre from Barnes, Hay lofts and Stables . . . insomuch that the very strawes blowne with the winde, and falling on hearbes, doe greatly annoy and harm them.

Of all the windes, for the benefite of the Garden, is the Southwest winde especially commended.

. . . the placing of a garden-ground near to a Fenne or Marrish [marsh], is everie where to be misliked and refused for the ayre thereabouts doth ingender either the Pestilence, or wicked vermin, much harming the garden-plot lying nigh to it.

If a well be lacking in the garden, then digge a deep pit, leveled in the bottome with bricke and lime to receive the raine water falling.

27

Flowers planted in raised beds. *The Gardener's Labyrinth*

Watering was clearly a problem. If no arrangements could be made, moisture could be retained by deep digging, 'three or foure foote the deeper, or lower'. Earlier in the century, labourers at Hampton Court had been paid for 'ladyng water out of ye Temmes to fyll the ponds in the night tymes'.

'The most commendable inclosure for everie garden plot, is a quickset hedge, made with brambles and white thorne.'

Formal arrangement of beds surrounded by a trellised balustrade—the whole garden contained by a wooden pallisade. *The Gardener's Labyrinth*

28

He recommends also mixed hedges of 'wilde Eglantine Bryars', brambles, gooseberries and barberries (*berberis*), and one made by planting elder trees 'three foot asunder' and filling the spaces with brambles. 'Within three yeares following [this will] grow to such a strength and surenesse, that the same will be able inough to defend the injuries both of the theefe and the beast.'

The diagrammatic Sun emphasises the point of the arbour. Turf seats and a table make this one of the earliest representations of outdoor living. *The Gardener's Labyrinth*

From The Gardener's Labyrinth *by Didymus Mountain, edition of 1586:*

Doves dung is ye best, because the same possesseth a mightie hoteness.

The dung also of the hen and other foules greatly commended for the sournesse, except ye dung of geese, ducks, and other waterfoules.

A commendation next is attributed to the Asses dung, in that the same beast for his leisurely eating, digesteth easier, and causeth the better dung.

The third in place is the Goates dung, after this both ye Oxe and Cow dung; next the Swines dung, worthier than the Oxen or Kine. The vilest and worst of all dungs after the opinion of the Greek writers of Husbandry, is the horse and moiles [mules].

The dung which men make (if the same be not mixed with the rabbith, or dust swept out of the house) is greatly mislyked, for that by nature it is hoter, and burneth the seedes sowne in that earth: so that this is not to be used, unlesse the grounde be a barren, gravelly or verie loose sand, lacking strength in it.

The mud also of running water, as the ditch or river, may bee employed instead of dung.

If no kinde of dung can be purchased, then in gravelly grounds it shall be best to dung the same with Chalke.

As touching remedies against the Frogges, which in the summer nyghtes are wont to be disquieters of the wearied husbandmen, by chyrping and loude noyse making, let the Husbandman burie in some banke fast by, the gaule of a Goat, the Frogs will not afterwarde gather in that place.

A Greek remedy against Caterpillars:
Take a few of the Caterpillars in the next Garden or Orchard, and seeth them in water with hearbe Dill, which being cold sprinkle on the hearbes or trees, or in such places where they be, and the same shall destroy them. But take verie diligent heede, that none of this water fall, either on your face or hands.

Longford Castle, Wiltshire, showing walled enclosures.

Artochoke reformeth the savour of the mouth.

Artochoke causeth urine and veneriall act.

Artochoke amendeth the hardness of making water and the rank savour of the armpits.

Artochoke strengtheneth the stomacke, & helpeth the privie places that men children may be conceived.

Borage procureth gladsomeness, it helpeth the giddiness and swimming of the head, the trembling and beating of the heart, it increaseth memorie, and removeth melancolie and the kings evil, it doth only comfort.

Carots amend a cold rheume, the paine of the stomacke, stopping of urine, and chollike, a drye cough, the hard fetching of breath, the fluxe of the head, remove wind, heat the stomacke, helpe the stopping of the liver, the vexing of the belly.

Elecampane putteth away yre and heavinesse, comforteth the heart, and sendeth forth the superfluous humours by urine; this causeth mirth.

Elecampane defendeth and preserveth the skin of the face, and like garnisheth the whole body with a continuall seemliness.

Lettuce procureth sleepe, causeth good bloude, helpeth digestion, looseth the belly, causeth plentifulness of milk in the breastes, sharpneth the sight, cooleth impostumes, helpeth the dropsy, cureth the shedding of sperm, procureth sleep being laid under the coverlet, and profiteth Cholericke persons.

Lettuce is noisome unto married men: it dulleth the sight of the eies. It abateth the venerealle acte, it harmeth the fleumaticke; the overmuch eating of Lettuce is as perilous as Hemlocke.

31

Balustrades, seats and garden pavilions, built about 1590, enclose the forecourt of Montacute House in Somerset.

The Roman Garden.
Courtyard of a house in
Pompeii.

A Mediaeval
Garden. From *The
Romance of the Rose*,
about 1475.

13 Broad bean and borage, with a thistle, an iris, a daisy and a strawberry.

14 Green hellbore and 'fleur de lys', with strawberry.

15 Thistle and teazle.

16 Cowslip corn cockle, with a pink.

17 Daffodil and gillyflower, a border pink.

18 Columbine and white campion.

From: A Herbal and Bestiary ABC, early 16th century.

He advises the 'gardnere' to be sure that '. . . the earth be neither hote and bare, nor leane by sande, lacking a mixture of perfite earth: nor the same founde to be wholly Chalke, nor naughtie sand: nor barraine gravell, nor of the glittering powder or dust of a leane stonie ground, nor the earth continuall moist . . .'

He suggests a framework of 'seemlie walkes and Alleis', some of grass and some that 'may cleanly be sifted over with river sand' to prevent 'the earth cleaving and clagging to the feet'. He gives instructions for 'beddes and seemely borders', which should be no more than 'three foote of breadth . . . that the weeders handes may well reach into the midell of the same'.

The Royal Charter to the Companie of Gardiners of London was received in 1606, and they had the power to inspect, and to destroy, any seeds or plants that were offered for sale, if they were unwholesome, dry, rotten, deceitful or unprofitable.

The frontispiece to Gerard's *Herbal* of 1597, showing raised beds.

33

A Visit to England, 1599:

Thomas Platter was born in Basel, when his father was seventy-five. His half-brother was Rector of the University. He visited England when he was twenty-five.

'On Sunday, September 26th, I and my party drove by coach through the borough of Tooting to see the royal palace of Nonsuch 12 English miles, or some reckon 10, from London.

'At the entrance to the garden is a grove called after Diana, the goddess. From here we came to a rock out of which natural water springs into a basin, and on this was portrayed with great art and life-like execution the story of how the three goddesses took their bath naked and sprayed Actaeon with water, causing antlers to grow upon his head, and of how his hounds afterwards tore him to pieces. Further on we came to a small vaulted temple, where was a fine marble table and mottoes were inscribed there . . .

'We next entered an arbour or pavilion where the queen [Elizabeth I, then aged sixty-six] sits during the chase in the park. Here she can see the game run past. Then through a wood in the gardens, with fine straight long alleys through it, fashioned in this wise. In the very densest part of the wood about here a great many trees are uprooted and cleared, within a breadth of some eighteen to twenty feet, along a straight course, so that there is a vista from one end to the other. And here and there they are partitioned off on either side with high boards, so that the balls may be played in the shade of these same alleys very pleasantly, as in an enclosed tennis court . . .

'From here we came to a maze or labyrinth surrounded by high shrubberies to prevent one passing over or through them. In the pleasure gardens are charming terraces and all kinds of animals—dogs, hares, all overgrown with plants, most artfully set out, so that from a distance, one would take them for real ones.'

At Hampton Court, he mentions that the first large forecourt is covered with grass. In the third court there was 'a fine large fountain wrought of white marble, with an excellent water work with which one may easily spray any ladies or others standing about, and wet them well'.

'At the entrance [to the garden] I noticed numerous patches where square cavities had been scooped, as for paving stones; some of these were filled with red brick-dust, some with white sand, and some with green lawn, very much resembling a chess-board. The hedges and surrounds were of hawthorn, bush firs, ivy, roses, juniper, holly, English or common elm, box and other shrubs, very gay and attractive.

'There were all manner of shapes, men and women, half men and half horse, sirens, serving-maids with baskets, French lilies and delicate crenellations all round made from dry twigs bound together and the aforesaid evergreen quick-set shrubs, or entirely of rosemary, all true to the life, and so cleverly and amusingly interwoven, mingled and grown together, trimmed and arranged picture-wise, that their equal would be difficult to find.'

Crispin de Passe's design for a summer garden. This is an early example of the architectural elaboration of the garden and it is exclusively planted with flowers. From the English edition of *Hortus Floridus* 1616

Isaac de Caus' design for Wilton (1615): the plan retains elements of the medieval garden but has begun to use the imported ideas of the Italian Renaissance.

*It is the purest of human pleasures; it is the greatest
refreshment to the spirits of man; without which buildings
and palaces are but gross handy-works: and a man shall
ever see that, when ages grow to civility and elegancy, men
come to build stately sooner than to garden finely; as if
gardening were the greater perfection.*

Sir Francis Bacon, Of Gardens, 1625

Plants continued to arrive from all over the world: sent as seeds and bulbs
by agents and consuls from as far afield as Tripoli, Aleppo and Goa;
brought back by ships' captains from the Straits of Magellan, the Cape of
Good Hope, Peru and China. In Sir William Cecil's garden in Holborn,
in the 1590s, he had a Judas tree and a laburnum, from southern Europe, and
a lilac from eastern Europe—all of recent introduction.

Some vegetables came in with the flowers, notably a new carrot,
described by Thomas Hill as being both red and yellow. The purple one
turned stews a very unpleasant colour and it has not been used in this
country since then. Changes in diet followed, not without misgivings. In
The Anatomy of Melancholy, Robert Burton wrote, in 1621:

> Amongst herbs to be eaten, I find gourds, cowcumbers, coleworts
> [brassicas], disallowed, but especially cabbage. It causeth troublesome
> dreams, and sends up black vapours to the brain . . . Some are of the
> opinion that all raw herbs and sallets breed melancholy blood, except
> bugloss and lettuce. Crato [a Roman writer] speaks against all herbs and
> worts, except borage, bugloss, fennel, parsley, dill, balm, succory . . .
> Crato disallows all roots, though some approve of parsnips and potatoes
> . . . Crato utterly forbids all manner of fruits, as pears, apples, plums,
> cherries, strawberries, nuts, medlars, serves [from the service tree]
> etc . . .

Sir Francis Bacon published his essay *Of Gardens* in 1625. His ideas are not
always very practical, but he does admit, at the end, that he has been
offering a 'platform', that is to say a plan or pattern, 'of a princely garden
. . . not a model, but some general lines of it; and in this I have spared for
no cost.'

The knot garden had grown more and more elaborate; and use was still
made of small evergreen bushes clipped into animal shapes. Bacon,
however, did not approve of this: 'As for the making of knots or figures

Two designs for knots from William Lawson's *The Country Housewife's Garden*, 1638.

with divers coloured earths, they be but toys; you may see as good sights many times in tarts. . . . I for my part do not like images cut in juniper or other garden stuff; they be for children.'

From The English Husbandman *by Gervase Markham, 1613:*

Knot gardens were now laid out in coloured earths as well as coloured plants. 'You shall make your yellow, either of a yellow clay usually to be had in almost every place, or the yellowest sand, or for want of both, of your Flanders Tile, which is to be bought of every Iron-munger or Chandelor: and any of these you must beat to dust. For your white you shall make it of the coarsest chalk beaten to dust, or of well-burnt plaster, or, for necessity, of lime, but that will soon decay. Your black is to be made of your best and purest coal-dust, well cleansed and sifted. Your red is to be made of broken useless bricks beaten to dust and well cleansed of spots. Your blue is to be made of white-chalk, and blacke coal dust well mixed together, till the black have brought the white to a perfect blueness.

'You shall upon the face of your quarter draw a plaine double knot . . . and you shall let it be more than a foote betwixt line and line (for in the largenesse consists much beauty) this knot being scored out, you shall rake Tiles, or tile shreds, and fixe them within the lines of your knot strongly within the earth. . . . Then betwixt your tiles, plant in every several thread flowers of one kinde and colour, as thus for example; in one thread plant your carnation gillyflower, in another your great white gillyflower, in another your mingle coloured gillyflower, and in another your blood-red gillyflower and so likewise . . . you may in this sort plant your several coloured hyacinths, your several coloured Dulippos [tulips] and many other Italian and French flowers. It shall appear like a knot made of divers coloured ribbons, most pleasing and most rare.'

William Lawson's *A New Orchard and Garden* (1618) shows the division into sections of the garden. One is a forecourt, four are for vegetables and fruit and only one is a knot garden.

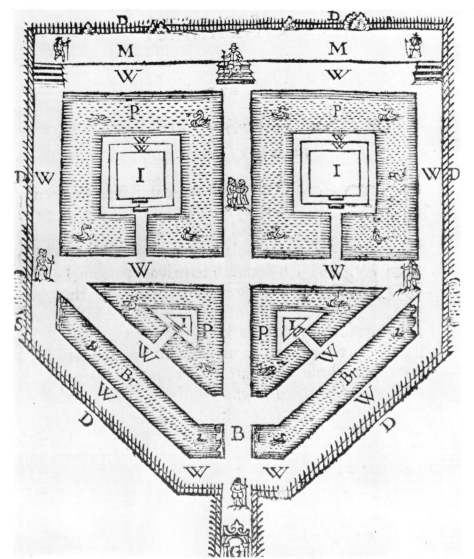

Formal arrangement of fish ponds, showing the islands which facilitated the netting of fish. Fishponds and dovecotes provided a readily accessible food supply. From Gervase Markham's *Cheap and Good Husbandry*, 1614

From Sir Francis Bacon's essay Of Gardens, *1625: his plan for a 'heath or desert', six acres in extent:*

'Trees I would have none in it, but some thickets made only of sweet-briar and honeysuckle, and some wild vine amongst; and the ground set with violets, strawberries, and primroses; for these are sweet, and prosper in the shade; and these to be in the heath here and there, not in any order. I like also little heaps, in the nature of mole-hills (such as are in wild heaths), to be set, some with wild thyme, some with pinks, some with germander that gives a good flower to the eye, some with periwinkle, some with violets, some with strawberries, some with cowslips, some with daisies, some with red roses, some with *Lilium convallium* [lily convally, lily-of-the-valley], some with sweet-williams red, some with bear's foot [the green hellebore], and the like low flowers, being withal sweet and sightly; part of which heaps to be with standards of little bushes pricked upon their top, and part without: the standards to be roses, juniper, holly, barberries (but here and there, because of the smell of their blossom), red currants, gooseberries, rosemary, bays, sweet-briar and such-like: but these standards to be kept with cutting, that they grow not out of course.'

The gallery of the enclosed garden has become '. . . a stately arched hedge; the arches to be upon pillars of carpenter's work, of some ten foot high and six foot broad. . . . Over the arches let there be an entire hedge of some four feet high, framed also upon carpenter's work; and upon the upper hedge, over every arch a little turret with a belly enough to receive a cage of birds; and over every space between the arches some other little figure, with broad plates of round coloured glass gilt, for the sun to play upon: but this hedge I intend to be raised upon a bank, not steep but gently sloped, of some six foot, set all with flowers.'

Bacon does not like aviaries nor, it appears, pools.

For aviaries, I like them not, except they be of that largeness as they may be turfed and have living plants and bushes set in them.
For fountains, they are a great beauty and refreshment; but pools mar all and make the garden unwholesome and full of flies and frogs.

The garden should not be less than thirty acres; his mount is thirty foot high, with a fine banqueting house with neat chimneys but not too much glass. The mount has three approaches, wide enough for four to walk abreast, and is right in the middle of the garden. At the end, there is a

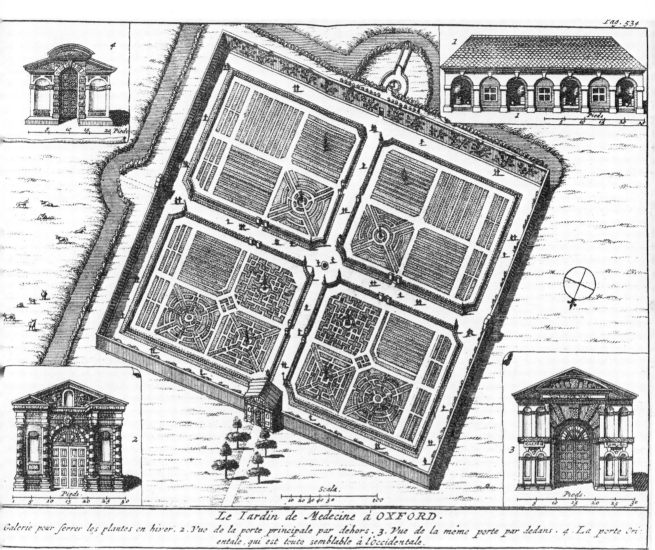

Le Jardin de Medecine à OXFORD.
Galerie pour serrer les plantes en hiver. 2. Vue de la porte principale par dehors. 3. Vue de la même porte par dedans. 4. La porte Orientale, qui est toute semblable à l'Occidentale.

smaller mount, 'to look abroad into the fields'. The close alleys, beneath the carpenter's work, are to be gravelled, the open ones are to be grassed. Beyond the garden there is to be a 'heath or desert' of six acres, carefully planted and maintained.

The first botanical garden was founded at this time, at Oxford. Elaborate Italian fountains and statues became fashionable, particularly in the Royal gardens. Travellers brought back seeds and bulbs almost as a matter of course; and one of the first great collections of foreign plants was made by the Tradescant family in Lambeth.

In 1629, John Parkinson published *Paradisus in Sole*, the title a punning translation into Latin of his own name, 'Park in Sun'. It contains detailed descriptions of the flowers he grew in his garden in Long Acre, and others observed in those of his friends, one of whom was John Tradescant.

Oxford Physic Garden was the first botanical garden in England. Begun in 1621, it had a formal layout for botanical specimens. Some of the gateways still exist.

41

The frontispiece for John Parkinson's *Paradisus in Sole*, published in 1629.

Narcissus from Parkinson:

1 The Great Spanish Bastard Daffodil
2 The Mountain Bastard Daffodil of divers kind
3 The Greater White Spanish Bastard Daffodil
4 The Lesser White Spanish Bastard Daffodil
5 The Six-Cornered Bastard Daffodil
6 John Tradescant's Great Rose Daffodil
7 Master Wilmer's Great Double Daffodil
8 The Great Spanish or Parkinson's Double Daffodil
9 The Greater Double French Daffodil
10 The Double English or Gerrard's Double Daffodil

Iris from Parkinson (The 'fleur de lys' of Heraldry):

1 The Great Turkey Flower de luce
2 The White Flower de luce
3 The variable Flower de luce
4 The Greater Dwarf Flower de luce

'Those flowers that have been usually planted in former times in Gardens of this Kingdome have by time and custome attained the name of English flowers, although most of them were never naturall of this our land, but brought from other Countries at one time or other, by those that tooke pleasure in them when they first saw them. . . .

'Thus have I, (in the following pages), showed you most of the English, as well as the Out-landish flowers, that are fit to furnish the knots, trailes, beds and borders of this Garden. . . .

'The four square forme is the most usually accepted with all, and doth best agree with any mans dwelling, being behinde the house, all the backe windows thereof opening into it.'

He mentions a small, low or dwarf kind of Box, 'called French or Dutch boxe. It will growe very thicke, and yet not require great tending, nor so much perish as any of the former [kinds of Box], and is onely received into the Gardens of those that are curious', by which he meant that it had been only recently introduced.

He lists more than a hundred daffodils, among which we find agapanthus, 'the strange Sea Daffodil', sprekelia, 'the Indian Daffodil with a red flower', and pancratium, 'the White Sea Bastard Daffodil'. There were thirty crocuses, a martagon lily from Canada and, from Peru, the giant sunflower, 'The Mervaile of Peru' [*Mirabilis jalapa*] and what we now call the nasturtium.

But tulips were the fashionable flowers of the time, brought from the Balkans, the Near and the Middle East. They hybridised freely and a new race of Florist's Tulips arose. They took three or four years to flower from seed. Among others, Parkinson mentions 'a strawe colour; a pale Orange colour; a Vermilion; a faire deep purple; a creame colour.'

'A white Duke, that is parted white and crimson flames, from the middle of each leaf [petal] to the edge.'

'A Dutchesse, that is like unto the Duke, but more yellow than red, with great yellow edges, and the red more or less circling the middle of the flower on the inside, with a large yellow bottome.'

Tulipomania was to sweep Holland in the 1630s, whole fortunes being given for a single bulb.

Hyacinths, Crown Imperials—known in at least one Puritan Oxford-shire village as Parliament Bells—fritillaries, the white jasmine, thirty different kinds of rose, thrifts, which he calls 'pinks'. The foxglove 'I leave to his wild habitation'; and 'the Honisuckle that groweth wild in every hedge, although it be very swete, yet doe I not bring it into my garden,

Cabbages from Parkinson:

1 Close Cabbage
2 Open Cabbage
3 Curled Savoy Colewort
4 Cole Flower

5 Curled Colewort
6 Changeable Curled Colewort
7 Cole Rape
8 Not given. Perhaps Kohl Rabi

but let it rest in his owne place, to serve their sense that travell by it, or have no garden.'

Of the honeysuckles that he did bring into his garden, some were native to North America, a new and valuable source of plants for the English Garden.

A Garden Gateway inserted in the wall of the forecourt at Kirby Hall by Inigo Jones.

PART TWO

A Pattern for Pleasure,
1660–1725

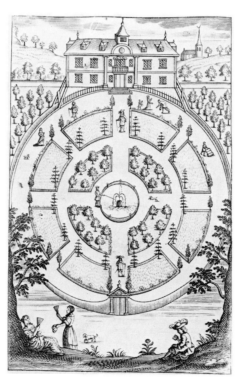

The Round Garden, from *Systema Horticultura*, or *The Art of Gardening*, by J. W. Gent.
(John Worlidge, 1683.)

'*A Gard'ners Work is never at an end; it begins with the Year, and continues to the next.*'

John Evelyn, who wrote those words, was born at Wotton in Surrey in 1620, the second son of a gentleman. He visited Holland in 1641. At the outbreak of the Civil War in 1642 he retired to Wotton, where he made 'a fish-pond, an island, and some other solitudes and retirements'. His example was followed by many other country gentlemen, who remained on their estates for the duration of the war and of the Commonwealth that followed it.

Evelyn, however, visited France in 1643, and seems to have remained abroad until 1646. The next year he married, and in this way acquired Sayes Court, at Deptford, where he retired completely after one more visit to France in 1649.

In 1653, 'I began to set out the oval garden at Sayes Court, which was before a rude orchard, and all the rest one entire field of 100 acres, without any hedge, except the hither holly-hedge joining to the bank of the mount walk'. The next month, February, 'I planted the orchard at Sayes Court; new moon, wind west'.

There are frequent references to the state of the moon in all gardening 'calendars' before this time. Very roughly we can say that they sowed and planted when the moon was waxing, picked and pruned when it was waning.

In 1654, he visited the Oxford Physic Garden where he found bamboo, olive trees, rhubarb, 'but no extraordinary curiosities'. In 1658, he published a translation from the French on the management of kitchen gardens.

By 1662, the fame of his garden at Sayes Court had spread and it was visited in that year by the King. His book *Sylva, A Discourse of Forest Trees* (1664) reached the Court, where it was taken seriously. It was to remain a standard work for more than a century. Early blast furnaces were denuding England of trees; but schemes of tree-planting were now started all over the country. It was this timber which was later to build Brittania's Navy.

'A timber tree is a merchant adventurer—you shall never know his worth till he be dead.' He deals fully with the native trees and gives instructions for their propagation, planting and maintenance. In the garden, he was a great advocate of hedges, and we may suppose that the hundred-acre garden at Sayes Court contained a great many.

19 A tulip, a garden anemone and a yellow violet.

20 A French marigold, Love-in-a-Mist and a garden pink.

21 A tulip, a narcissus and a larkspur.

22 A tulip, a 'blue convolvulus' and a gladiolus.

Garden Flowers of the Stuart period, painted by Alexander Marshall (1639–1682).

23 Cheveley Park, Newmarket. Painting by Jan Siberechts, 1681

24 (*Below*) Llanerch, Denbighshire, painted in 1662.

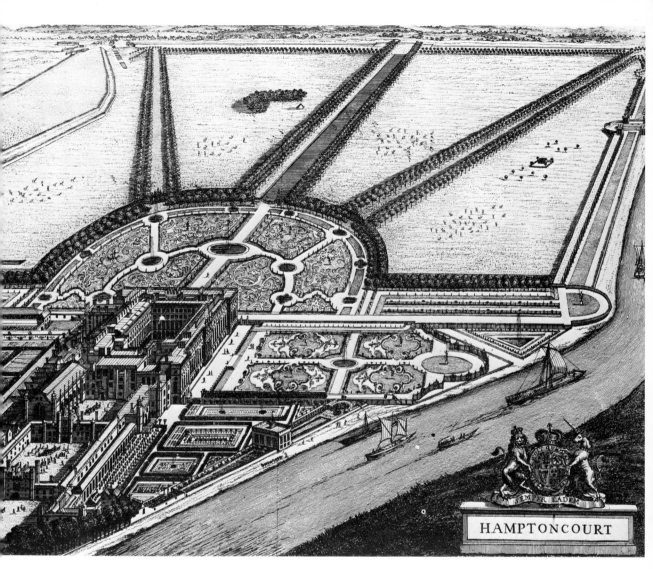

HAMPTONCOURT

André Le Nôtre and the English Garden

King Charles II was first cousin to Louis XIV of France. His mother, Queen Henrietta Maria, spent the years of the Commonwealth at the French Court, where she was visited by him. He also spent time in Holland where his sister Mary lived, widow of the Prince of Orange and mother of the future King William III.

Claude Mollet was the Head Gardener at the Tuileries in Paris, in 1613, the same year that his wife stood godmother to André Le Nôtre, son of one of the other gardeners.

André Mollet, one of Claude's four sons, was summoned to England in 1620 to introduce the New French Style, but little seems to be known of his work at that time. He worked in Holland and Sweden and his book, *The Pleasure Garden*, was published in French, Swedish and German in 1651, in English in 1670. In 1661 he was working as a Royal Gardener in St. James's Park, with his nephew Gabriel.

Hampton Court Palace, about 1690. The garden, as designed by Daniel Marot for King William III. Drawn by Leonard Knyff, engraved by Johannes Kip. A certain schizophrenia existed in the English Garden at this time. While it was neither wholly Dutch, nor wholly French, it was not English either.

49

Meanwhile, André Le Nôtre had risen to be Head Gardener at the Tuileries, succeeding his father in 1637. One of his first major works was to lay out the garden at Vaux-le-Vicomte, as we can see it today, in 1650. He became Royal Gardener to King Louis XIV but his work at Versailles did not begin until 1661.

When Charles II regained his Kingdom in 1660, one of the first things he did was to ask King Louis if he might borrow Le Nôtre. Permission was given, though Le Nôtre was 'very occupied at Fontainebleau'; but, there is no record that Le Nôtre ever came to England.

The garden in St. James's Park, which King Charles began within weeks of his return, was therefore laid out in the style of Claude Mollet, who had made great use of the 'patte d'oie' or goose-foot, a number of avenues radiating from a semi-circle, like the webbed foot of a goose, or the three middle fingers of the human hand, fanned out.

There could be three, or five, or seven radiations, either avenues or canals. In St. James's Park a canal was made, 2800 feet long and 100 feet wide, apparently centred on the Banqueting House. It was the central radiation; the others were avenues of acacias, *Robinia pseudo-acacia*, recently introduced from North America.

At Hampton Court, King Charles laid down the Long Water, a simple rectangular canal, originally with a double row of lime trees down each side. At Greenwich, for which he had wanted the help of Le Nôtre, he seems only to have planted the park with elms; he referred to it as 'a piece of as barren ground as is in England'. In a map dated 1695, space appears for 'a parterre by Le Nôtre', but it does not seem to have been made. Le Nôtre could have sent a design for the park at Greenwich, but if he did, it has disappeared, though the design for the parterre still exists. The work that was actually done at Greenwich appears to owe nothing to him.

The first English gardener at St. James's was John Rose, appointed on the death of André Mollet in 1665. He had been sent by the Earl of Essex to study in France with André Le Nôtre, but he does not appear to have altered the layout of St. James's in any way.

When William III became King, he employed Daniel Marot, a pupil of André Le Nôtre, who had already designed for him the garden at Het Loo, in Holland, to alter the gardens at Hampton Court. This garden was again altered, if not precisely destroyed, by Queen Anne, on the death of William III. Many other similarly elaborate gardens met the same fate.

It is therefore very difficult to determine, precisely, what influence André Le Nôtre had on the evolution of the English Garden.

Of the yew, he says: 'Being three years old, you may transplant them, and form them into standards, knobs, walks, hedges &c. in all which works they succeed marvellous well, and are worth our patience for their perennial verdure and durableness. I do again name them for hedges, preferable, for beauty and a stiff defence, to any plant I have ever seen, and may, upon that account, without vanity, be said to have been the first who brought it into fashion . . . braving all the efforts of the most rigid winter which cypresses cannot weather.'

One might notice here that the rigid winter of 1683–84 killed off all the Italian cypresses growing in England; they have been very little planted since. The cypresses that one sees today, too big, too small, too wide, too tall, coarsely textured and almost always planted wrongly, nearly all come from North America.

Another hedge that Evelyn introduced was the alaternus [one of the Buckthorns], 'which we have lately received from the hottest parts of Languedoc. [It] thrives with us in England as if it were an indigene and natural. . . . I have had the honour to be the first who brought it into use and reputation in this kingdom.' Phillyrea, from the Mediterranean, he mentions as being as hardy as holly; both make excellent hedges. 'The Hawthorn', however, is 'indeed the very best of common hedges.' Tamarisk makes a good hedge, but is not evergreen; 'The American Yucca is a hardier plant than we take it to be. . . . Why should it not make one of the best and most ornamental fences in the world for our gardens?' 'Hornbeam, Elme, Beech, make excellent, tall, and thick strong hedges, planted in single row onely & kept clip'd.'

John Rose, the Royal Gardener, presenting to Charles II the first pineapple grown in England.

From John Evelyn's Kalendarium Hortense, *1664:*

March: Sow in the beginning Endive, Succory, Leeks, Radish, Beets, Chard-Beet, Scorzonera, Parsneps, Skirrets [a root vegetable to be displaced by the potato].
                    Sow also Parsly, Sorrel, Bugloss, Borage, Chervil, Sellery, Smalladge, Alisanders.
                    Sow also Lettuce, Onions, Garlick, Orach [an alternative to spinach], Purslain, Turneps, monthly Pease.
                    Sow also Carrots, Cabbages, Cresses, Fennel, Marjoran, Basil, Tobacco.
        Turn your Fruit in the Room where it lies, but open not yet the windows.
        Some of the hardiest Evergreens may now be transplanted, especially if the weather be moist and temperate.

[In April, he has an arrangement of straw mattresses on cradles of hoops to protect seedlings from hail, rain and sun. The oranges can now be watered, at blood heat. 'Let the water stand in the Sun till it grow tepid.']

May: Observe the Mulberry-tree, when it begins to put forth and open the leaves, (be it earlier or later) bring your Oranges &c boldly out of the Conservatory.
                    Cleanse vines of exuberant Branches and Tendrels.

July: You may feed your Vines with Blood, Sweet, and mingled with Water.
                    Have still an Eye to the weeding and cleansing part; begin the work of Haughing [hoeing] as soon as ever they begin to peep; you will rid more in a few Hours, than afterwards in a whole Day; whereas neglecting it till they are ready to sow themselves, you do but stir and prepare for a more numerous Crop of these Garden-Sinns: I cannot too often inculcate and repeat it.

August: Clip roses now done bearing.

September: Sow Lettuce, Radish, Spinage, Parsneps, Skirrets &c Caullyflowers, Cabbages, Onions &c Scurvy grass Anniseeds.
                    About Michaelmas (sooner or later, as the Season directs) the weather faire, and by no means foggie, retire your choice Greens, and rarest Plants (being dry) into your Conservatory.

October: Moon now decreasing, gather Winter-fruit that remains. Plant and plash quick-sets.
                    You may yet sow Genoa Lettuce, which will last all the

Winter, especially under Glass-bells with a little Straw over them, when the hard Frosts come; but then touch them not till they thaw, lest you crack the Glasses.

November: Take up your Potatoes.

[He offers a picture of A New Conservatory, or Green-house, glass on one side only and says it must not be more than 12 or 13 feet deep.]

From Evelyn's Directions to the Gardiner at Says Court:

Notes for the Kitchin-Garden: Chervill is handsom and proper for the edging of Kitchin Garden beds.

Notes for the Physic-Garden: Physical plants should be set in Alphabetical order, for the better retaining them in memorie: [He lists 161, including Dandelion, still in use as a salad plant, rhubarb, tobacco and woad.]

Notes for the Coronary Garden (The Flower Garden): Lavender Cotton clip'd makes a pretty hedge or bordure for a Flower garden, and may be maintained a foot high.

Transplanting: Plant when the wind is south or west. Plant very little deeper than it grew before. You cannot plant too early in the Autumn, all such trees as loose their leaves in Winter. But plant not Ever-greenes 'til the beginning of April, when you perceive them begin to shoot.

The best use of Horse dung (fresh made) is to raise the Hot-bed. Cow-dung well rotted, not too dry, is best for hot, dry, leane & sandy grounds; it should be gathred in the Autumn, and saved in heapes, to be broken and mingled afterwards.

Pidgeons & dung of poultry is excellent when cold, and well tempered & rotted with mould. Use it at the beginning of Winter: especially for Asparagus and Strawberries.

Pidgeons and sheepes dung infused in Water is excellent for Oranges, choice greenes, & indeed any Fruite.

The scouring of muddy-ponds, & where cattell drinke and stand, is good for all plants.

The scowring of privies & sinkes so well dried and made sweete, well mixed with fresh earth so as to retain no heady scent, is above all other excellent for Oranges & the like choice fruits.

The best remedy against Garden earth-wormes, is well to water the places infected with water wherein potash (soape) have been dissolved, & well stirred.

Poultrie & Catts are to be hinder'd from scraping and basking by laying brambles, & holy-bushes on the beds.

Sow Tulip-seede shallow, & under the bed lay a slate, broad stone or board under the Earth about 2 inches, & the second yeare plant the young seedlings, do the same the 3d year this keapes the bulbe from sinking, which else they will yearely do, which hinders their bearing for many years.

Thuya, which he called *Arbor-vitae*, the arbutus, the bay and the cherry laurel he recommends as 'grove trees', as opposed to forest trees. Groves were little woods of small trees. Of the cherry laurel, he says: 'I dare pronounce it to be one of the most proper and ornamental trees for walks and avenues of any growing.' Of the native shrubs, he mentions the following as being suitable for groves: furse, broom, elder, the spindle tree, dogwood and the wayfaring tree.

Elsewhere, he refers to, as 'Not-Vulgar Trees', the plane, both the 'oriental or Zinar', and the 'Occidental'—the probable parents of the London Plane—'the Larch, the tulip tree or Virgin Maple' [*Liriodendron tulipifera*], the Cork-tree [*Quercus suber*], the Spanish-Oake [probably *Quercus falcata*], the White-Mulberrie, the Virginian Wallnut, the Lentiscus [*Pistacia lentiscus*, also called the Mastic Tree] and the acacia [*Robinia*].'

'The Constantinople, or Horse-Chesnut, is beautifull for great walks & Avenues, but should be planted where the winds come not fiercely, which is apt to take off whole branches.'

The poet Edmund Waller's garden at Hall Barn, near Beaconsfield.

The garden begun by the poet Edmund Waller at this time, at Hall Barn near Beaconsfield, is still there today. One can see the system of linked avenues, not radiating from a semi-circle but from one of the points of view, and a rectangular sheet of water slightly too broad to be called a canal. It exudes the great calm that this kind of garden must have had. At Hall Barn, too, Waller 'plashed' his trees, cutting the avenue trees back on one side to make, as it were, a gigantic hedge.

Waller began his garden in 1651, after travelling with John Evelyn through Italy and France

In 1662, 'John Rea gent' published *Flora, Ceres & Pomona*— respectively, the Roman goddesses of Flowers, Corn and Fruit. In it, he offered the experience of 'fourty years' and 'certain and assured directions how to set, make grow, increase, and preserve each particular; as also for the raising of new Varieties, not taken out of simple Books (the Publishers and Retainers of many Untruths) but learned from my practical Experience.' He has not 'inserted any of those notorious lies I have frequently found in Books of this Subject, but in plain English terms, set down the truth in every particular'.

It is knowledge that begets Affection, and Affection increaseth Knowledge. . . . It is chiefly that, which hath made my Flowers and Trees to flourish, though planted in a barren Desart [his house was at Kinlet near Bewdly in Worcestershire], and hath brought me to the knowledge I now have in Plants and Planting.

55

An avenue of plashed
trees leading to the
obelisk which commem-
orated the completion of
the garden by Waller's
grandson, about 1730.
(Hall Barn)

Trinity College,
Cambridge, in 1688,
showing trees and shrubs
planted in raised beds
within walled enclosures.

A Beech Walk,
hedged with cherry
laurel, leading to a temple.
(Hall Barn)

The formal water at
Hall Barn today.

I have known many Persons of Fortune pretend much affection to
Flowers, but very unwilling to part with anything to purchase them;
yet if obtained by begging, or perhaps by stealing, contented to give
them entertainment.

The garden he describes is still the garden of Parkinson, but the proportion
is different. He offers an illustration of the layout for a vegetable garden, a
simple arrangement of rectangles. There is no sign of France in this
particular Desart.

I have seen many Gardens of the new model, in the hands of unskilful
Persons, with good Walls, Walks, and Grass-plots; but in the most
essential ornaments so deficient, that a green Medow is a more
delightful object; there Nature alone, without the aid of Art, spreads
her verdant Carpets, spontaneously embroidered with many pretty
Plants, and pleasing Flowers, far more inviting than such an immured
Nothing. And as Noble Fountains, Grotto's, Statues &c. are excellent
Ornaments, and marks of Magnificence; so all such dead Works in
Gardens, ill done, are little better than Blocks in the way to intercept the
sight, but not at all able to satisfy the understanding. A choice collection
of living Beauties, rare Plants, Flowers and Fruits, are indeed the
Wealth, glory and delight, of a Garden.

Fourscore yards square for the Fruit, and Thirty for the Flower
Garden, will be enough for a Nobleman: but for the private
Gentleman, Forty for the one, and Twenty for the other.

The most 'graceful Grounds' for a garden is an entire level; hanging grounds, he says, seldom make handsome gardens. He gives instructions for making rails for the flower borders, that is to say a board on edge raising the soil five inches above the level of the ground, in the mediaeval way. He has 'pole-hedges', trellis, of pyracantha and phillyrea, celastrus and alaternus, and tells how to make roses shoot in such a way that they cover the trellis (these were not the climbing roses that we know today). He has a special border—by which we should understand a border of raked earth, or gravel—'intended to place Pots upon'. There is no mention of a mount in his garden, but the arbour that might have been on it is still with us. It has been moved.

It will require to have in the middle of one side of this Flower-garden a handsome Octangular Somer-house, roofed in every way, and finely painted with landskips, and other conceits, furnished with seats about, and a Table in the middle; which serveth not onely for delight and entertainments, to sit in, and behold the beauties of the Flowers, but for many other necessary purposes; as, to put the Roots of Tulips, and other Flowers in, as they are taken up, upon Papers, with the names upon them, until they be dried.

He does the savage Hawthorn teach
To bear the Medlar and the Pear;
He bids the rustick Plum to rear
A noble Trunk, and be a Peach.
              Abraham Cowley.

The first major nursery was founded in 1681, in John Evelyn's words, 'at Brampton-Park near Chelsey, under the Direction of that excellent Gard'ner Mr. London, worthy of his Royal Title'. More or less occupying the site of the present South Kensington Museums, it extended as far as Hogmire Lane, now called Gloucester Road.

Melbourne Hall, Derbyshire—the only garden by Henry Wise to survive the destruction of formal gardens in the period of Capability Brown. It was begun in 1696. *Left*: Arbour of wrought iron by Robert Bakewell. *Right*: Fountain in circular basins.

George London was a pupil of John Rose, the gardener at St. James's. He started the business with three other partners, and the first foreman was Leonard Meager, whose book *The English Gardner* went through several editions between 1670 and 1710.

In 1687, London was joined by Henry Wise. They worked at Chatsworth where, in the same year, the Earl of Devonshire retired to re-build, an excuse for absenting himself from the Court of James II. London and Wise worked also at Blenheim, where they employed Charles Bridgeman and Stephen Switzer, of whom we shall hear later, and at Melbourne, in Derbyshire, where some of their work can still be seen. They were the Royal Gardeners to Queen Anne. The maze they made at Hampton Court is thought to have been originally of hornbeam; and they also worked at Windsor. Henry Wise seems to have remained in London, looking after the nursery and paying his respects to royalty; George London rode round the countryside from one great house to another, advising the nobility and gentry on the spot.

John Worlidge, the second edition of whose *Systema Horticultura or the Art of Gardening in three books by J. W. Gent* was published in 1683, offers us a clear picture of what the provincial gentleman, who could not afford to consult George London, for instance, was doing on his own. He says that there is not 'a Noble or pleasant Seat in England but hath its gardens for pleasure and delight; scarce an Ingenious Citizen that by his confinement to a Shop, being denied the privilege of having a real Garden, but hath his boxes, pots or other receptacles for Flowers, Plants, etc. . . . there is scarce a Cottage in most of the Southern Parts of England but hath its proportionable Garden, so great a delight do most men take in it.'

The gulf between those who lived in London and those who did not was already a large one. The following comment is therefore very interesting:

> The new mode of Gravel Walks and Grass-plots, is fit only for such Houses or Palaces, that are scituated in Cities and great Towns, although they are now become presidents for many stately Country Residencies, where they have banish'd out of their Gardens Flowers, the Miracles of Nature, and the best Ornaments that ever were discovered to make a Seat pleasant. But it's hoped that this new, useless, and unpleasant mode, will like many other vanities grow out of Fashion.

He offers 'a rude draught' of a round and a square garden. Simplicity appears to be his aim, and common sense his guide.

> If your Ground you intend for a Garden, lye on the side of a Hill, your Walks may be made the one above the other, and be as Terraces the one to the other; the declining sides of them, being either of Grass or planted with fruit.

> If your House stand on the side of a Hill, and you must make your Garden either above it or below it, then make your Garden below it, for it is much more pleasant to view a Garden under the Eye than above it, and to descend into a Garden and ascend to a House, than on the contrary.

> . . . endeavour to make your principal Entrance into your Garden, out of the best Room in your house . . .

We should perhaps remember that the countryside of England was still relatively wild. Great drainage schemes were being carried out. As early as 1670, Evelyn had recorded that fashionable house-parties would sometimes go to watch a river being made more navigable or a fen being drained. In 1683, a country gentleman, like John Worlidge, might still find himself obliged to do something of the same sort.

> It is not unusual to raise a Mount with the waste Earth or Rubbish . . . whereon you may erect a Pleasure or Banquetting-House or such like place of Repose.
>
> Arbours, Benches and Seats are very necessary, being present expedients for them that are weary; but that which crowns the pleasures of a Garden is a place of repose, where neither Wind, Rain, Heat, nor Cold can annoy you.
>
> This small Edifice, usually term'd a Pleasure-house or Banquetting-house, may be made at some remote Angle of your Garden: For the more remote it is from your House, the more private will you be from the frequent disturbances of Your Family and Acquaintance.
>
> A fair Stream or Current flowing through or near your Garden, adds much to the Glory and Pleasure of it.

Other remarks presage the garden of the eighteenth century. Worlidge has a small section on grottoes, says that 'Statues are commendable in the midst of Fountains and green Squares and Groves, and at the end of obscure Walks'. He mentions that the Ancient Romans adorned their gardens with statues and that this 'vanity', although excusable, is descended on the Italians; however, this 'mode of adorning Gardens with curious Workmanship is now become English'.

> 'Other ancient Ornaments of a Garden are Flower-Pots, which painted white and placed on Pedestals, either on the ground or in a streight line on the edges of your Walks, or on your Walls, or at the corners of your Squares, are exceeding pleasant . . .' He recommends an aviary and says also:

> But if the Place you live in be so dry,
> That neither Springs nor Rivers they are nigh,
> Then at some distance from your Garden make,
> Within the gaping Earth a spacious Lake.

From Systema Horticultura or The Art of Gardening in three books
Second Edition 1683 by J. W. Gent (John Worlidge):

'Of Walls:
Next unto the Brick, Stone Walls are preferred, the Square hewn Stone out of the Quarry, especially Sand or Free-Stone, is the best, the cold white Stone like unto Chalk or Lime-Stone is not so good. The Rough Heath-Stone or Burre is very dry and warm, but by its unevenness is unconvenient to tack Trees against, unless you disperse here and there in the Building some small squares of Timber, or Brickbats, in the joynts whereof Nails will enter and take. Flints are very cold and uneven joynted, and therefore the worst of all Stone for a Garden Fence.

In many places where Stone is dear, and Brick scarce, and Lime and Sand not near, Walls are often made by a Compost of Earth and Straw tempered with it. This Earth must be either of a clayish nature, or have a little mixture of Clay in it, it must be well wrought and mixed long with Dung or Straw, which serves to hold it together until it be thoroughly dry; and then according to the skill of the Workman, wrought up into a Wall and covered with Thatch, being not able to bear a more weighty Coping.

Of Grotto's:
It is a place that is capable of giving you so much pleasure and delight, that you may bestow not undeservedly what cost you please on it, by paving it with Marble, or immuring it with Stone or Rockwork, either natural or artificially resembling the Excellencies of Nature. The Roof may be made of the same supported with Pillars of Marble, and the Partitions made of Tables of the same.

Here follows a description of Several Fountains:
  I The Ball raised by a Spout of Water.
 II The Water representing a double Glass, the one over the other.
III A Dragon or such like, casting Water out of its mouth, as it runs round on the Spindle.
 IV A Crown casting Water out of several Pipes as it runs round.
  V A Statue of a Woman, that at the turning of a private Cock, shall cast Water out of her Nipples into the Spectators Faces.
 VI The Royal Oak with Leaves, Acorns, and Crowns dropping, and several small spouts round the top.

To have Roses until Christmas, you may plant the monthly Rose in some Niech of your South-wall, and you will have Rose buds fresh and fair in October, and in mild winters in November, which by shutters artificially made may be defended from the cold (sometimes admitting the Sun) until Christmas, you may add artificial warmth if you please. I have had fair rose buds in November with young by them, which might have been thus preserved.'

The detailed gardening knowledge of men like John Rea and John Worlidge was not to be required by the generations that immediately succeeded them, their preoccupation being with Taste. We may hope that their expertise continued to be respected in the kitchen gardens of the great houses, which were laid out as they suggested right into the present century.

'A great quantety of the Red Coralina goosbery'

The Glorious Revolution of 1688 brought to the throne King William and Queen Mary, a grandson and a granddaughter of King Charles I, who ruled as joint Monarch. The Queen introduced a fashion for Indian fabrics—described by Daniel Defoe as 'East-India Callicoes, Masslapatan Chints, Atlasses, and fine-painted Callicoes'—and for Chinese porcelain and pottery; the King had a passion for painting and gardening.

Again according to Defoe, 'The King began with the Gardens at Hampton-Court and Kensington, and the Gentlemen followed every where, with such Gust [enthusiasm] that the alteration is indeed wonderful thro' the whole Kingdom.' The flower, in process of being 'banished', to use John Worlidge's word, made its appearance inside as a motif for wood-carving, plasterwork, ironwork, embroidery and carpets, and as the sole subject of paintings.

Kensington Palace, about 1690. Knyff and Kip.

25 Pierrepont House, Nottingham. A garden laid out in the 1680s. Unknown Dutch Painter.

26 Dunham Massey, Cheshire. Painting by Adrian van Diest, 1696.

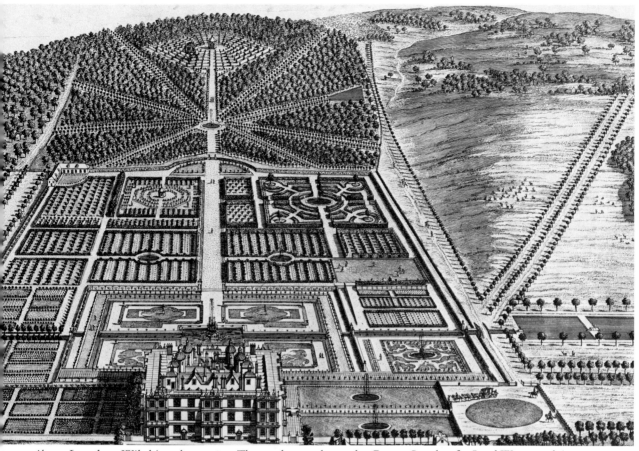

Above: Longleat, Wiltshire, about 1690. The garden was begun by George London for Lord Weymouth in 1685. Knyff and Kip. *Below*: Badminton, Gloucestershire, about 1690. Knyff and Kip.

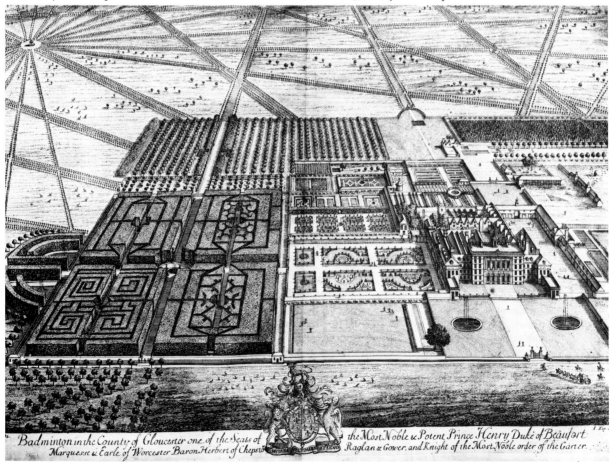

Badminton in the County of Gloucester one of the Seats of the Most Noble & Potent Prince Henry Duke of Beaufort Marquesse & Earle of Worcester Baron Herbert of Chepsto Raglan & Gower, and Knight of the Most Noble order of the Garter.

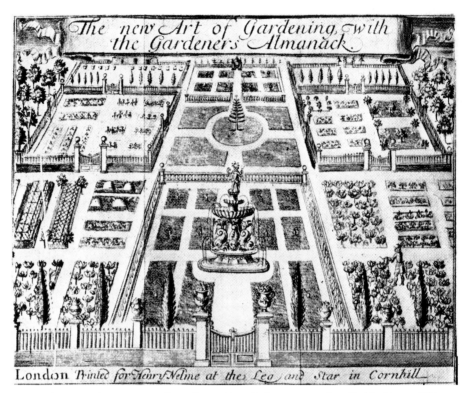

The new Art of Gardening, with the Gardener's Almanack.

London *Printed for Henry Nelme at the Leo and Star in Cornhill*

Leonard Meager's *New Art of Gardening* (1697) shows a garden divided into different compartments by architectural features, walls, balustrades and gateways.

Celia Fiennes, who rode 'through England on a Side Saddle in the time of William and Mary', was a lady of solid Roundhead ancestry: her grandfather was reported to have made of Banbury the most Puritan town in England. She was born in Wiltshire in 1662, was a non-Conformist, not subject to flights of fancy and the fact that she made her journeys at all says much for the state of the nation. In the journal she wrote, she offers valuable glimpses of the gardens that she saw

At Chatsworth:
... by the Grove stands a fine Willow tree, the leaves barke and all looks very naturall, and all on a sudden by turning a sluce it raines from each leafe and from the branches like a shower, it being made of brass and pipes to each leafe but in appearance is exactly like any Willow; beyond this is a bason in which are the branches of two Hartichocks Leaves which weeps at the end of each leafe into the bason.

Above: The spectacular siting of Powys Castle on the borders of England and Wales demanded a different kind of solution. The Terraced Gardens, begun about 1700, have fortunately remained, despite Capability Brown's suggestion that they should be levelled.

Below: The 19th and 20th centuries have managed to destroy the formal garden at the foot of the terraces and have planted an inappropriate shrub border on the lower terrace.

A Perspective View of POWES CASTLE in the County of Montgomery.

Westbury-on-Severn.
The wall on the public
road was pierced with
iron balustrading to allow
views of the garden to be
seen by passers-by.

At Woburn:

The Gardens are fine, there is a large bowling green with 8 arbours kept cut neatly, and seates in each, there is a seat up in a high tree that ascends from the green [the lawn] 50 steps, that commands the whole parke ... there are 3 large Gardens, fine gravell walks and full of fruite—I eate a great quantety of the Red Coralina [Carolina] goosbery which is a large thin skinn'd goosebery—the walks are one above another with stone steps: in the square just by the dineing room window is all sorts of pots of flowers and curious greens.

The word 'greens' is used at this time to denote almost any evergreen plant. 'Curious greens' would have been exotic plants—oranges, oleanders, possibly bay. They spent the winter in greenhouses. Elsewhere the word is used of clipped evergreens, holly, myrtle, box and yew, and there were others, not specified, which grew up walls.

68

The garden at Westbury-on-Severn was begun around 1700 and shows a use of formal water and walled enclosures, after the Dutch manner.

Still at Woburn:

. . . [you] pass under an arch into a Cherry garden, in the midst of which stands a figure of stone resembling an old weeder woman used in the garden, and my Lord would have her Effigie which is done so like and her clothes so well that at first I tooke it to be a real living body; on the other side of the house is another large Garden severall gravell walks one above another, and on the flatts are fish ponds the whole length of the walke.

At Durdans, in Surrey, a house built largely from the materials of Nonsuch Palace:

. . . looks nobly in a fine park pailed round, severall rows of trees in the front of all sorts, lofty and some cut piramidy some sugar loafe or rather like a mushroom top . . . two middle walks run up to a double mount which cast the garden into 3 long grass walks which are also very broad, with 3 flower potts . . . the long gravell walke to the right hand runns acrosse the mount to a thicket that enters the grove and is lost . . . high trees cut up to the top and with heads which close in an arch; in the middle is long white seats . . . you enter a space paved and open arch'd round in seates like a court, and thence you enter the grotto, an arch entirely dark, but at the entrance it is so large as 6 arched seates, and between, carved stone very fine of all sorts of flowers figures fruites, the pillars or peers pretty broad; this ran up to a summerhouse at the end, which is grown over with greens cut smooth.

There was a maze, a large square pond 'in nature of a canall' and flower pots painted blue and red.

These were the great houses. At Epsom, Celia Fiennes visits three much smaller ones. It was a time when spas were opening all over England, where people went, for their health, to drink the waters of natural springs. The 'Nobility and Gentry' went to Tunbridge; the 'Common People' chiefly to 'Dullwich and Stretham', according to Defoe, but also to Hampstead and Barnet, according to Celia Fiennes. The 'Merchants and Rich Citizens' went to Epsom, and clearly built houses for themselves there.

At Epsom, 'the Company', as Celia Fiennes called them, enjoyed, as 'a little diversion', the 'raceing of boyes, or rabets, or piggs', and at the house of Mrs. Rooth, in New Inn Lane, she found:

> . . . apricock, peach, plumb, necktarine, which spread [were espaliered or fan-trained], but not very high, between each is a cherry stript up to the top and spreads then composeing an arch over the others . . . this garden is the breadth of the dwelling-house, the dineing roome and drawing roome look into it . . . two mounts cut smoothe, between is a canall, these mounts are severall steps up under which are ice houses.

> Mrs. Steevens has a very pretty neat house and gardens . . . here are six grass walks three and three, guarded by dwarfe fruite trees . . . iron pallisadoes painted and gilt tops with gates leading to another garden of grass cut in shapes and knotts with flowers and all sorts of greens cut in shapes, with paths of gravel to form them, on the left side a coddling hedge secures a walke of orange and lemmon trees in perfection . . . in the green garden was a large alloes plant and all sorts of perpetualls as well as annuals.

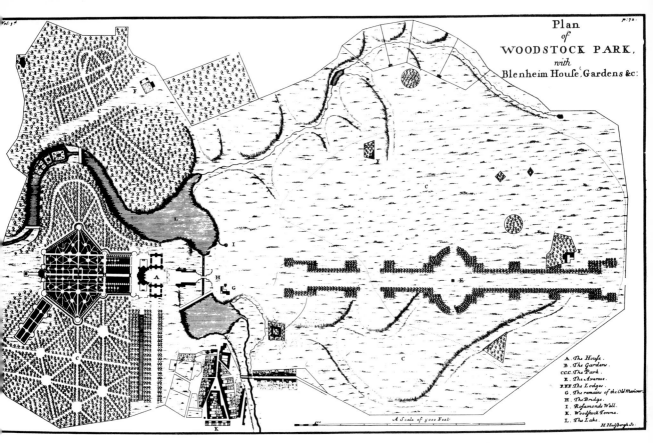

A. The House.
B. The Garden.
CCC. The Park.
E. The Avenue.
FFF. The Lodges.
G. The remains of the Old Manour.
H. The Bridge.
I. Rosamonds Well.
K. Woodstock Towne.
L. The Lake.

A Scale of 5000 Feet

H. Hulsbergh Sc:

Blenheim Palace, Oxfordshire. Wise's plan showing the great formal garden to the south of the palace, with its walks and bastions (derived from plans of fortifications designed by Vauban for Louis XIV's campaigns) providing a proper base for the building. The whole design has a military flavour suitable for the great Duke of Marlborough, with the splendid approach avenue. The plan also shows the separation of the kitchen garden from the surroundings of the house. Of all Capability Brown's alterations to the gardens of his predecessors, few were more disastrous than his destruction of the garden at Blenheim. The vast palace now sits on a lawn which, visually, does not support its weight.

Left: A more modest house, in John Lawrence's *Gentlemen's Recreation* of 1716, shows a concentration on the utilitarian aspect of the garden. The garden walls and grassed areas are taken up with fruit trees, and he has emphasised the aspect of the garden by showing a compass point in the centre. *Right*: Thomas Fairchild's *City Gardener* of 1721 shows an early example of greenhouses. The large tubs contain 'exoticks'.

At another house, there was a border of strawberries, punctuated with clipped evergreens. These would still have been the native wild strawberry, or perhaps the Great Bohemia Strawberry or the Prickly Strawberry, both of which were mentioned by Parkinson.

Nearby, at Beddington, Daniel Defoe, in his *Tour through the Whole of England and Wales*—made at about this time, though not published until 1724—found: '. . . the only Standard Orange-trees in England, and have moving Houses to cover them in the Winter; they are loaded with Fruit in the Summer, and the Gardners told us, they have stood in the Ground where they now grow above 80 years.'

Oranges and lemons were usually grown in large tubs and were moved into specially made buildings, called Orangeries, for the winter. There was also another kind of hothouse, called a Stove, which housed various other 'choice greens' during the winter.

The Marks of the Scissars

Most of the gardening books of this time were direct translations from the French and one of these was *The Theory and Practice of Gardening* by John James, which was 'done from the French original', of A. J. d'Argenville (1709), and it was published in London in 1712.

It gives us a very complete picture of the French garden of the time, although it is impossible to tell how many gardens were made in England entirely in this style. One of its most important features was the parterre, a development of the knot. The different strands of the Knot Garden always intertwined, and the outline was always square. The Parterre Garden was made up of different shapes divided from one another (from the Latin word *partire*, to divide, according to John James) and filled with grass, or gravel, or earth with regularly placed shrubs, or equally regularly placed flowers.

Warbrook, Hampshire. John James's own garden. Not only did he translate '*The Theory and Practice of Gardening*', but he was also an expert in 'hydraulics'.

Design for a Labyrinth, from *The Theory and Practice of Gardening*.

Design for three parterres, from *The Theory and Practice of Gardening*.

A Parterre after y^e English manner

A Parterre of Cutwork for Flowers

A Parterre of Orange Trees.

In the Introduction, he says that:

... our Woods and Groves, our Grass and Gravel, which are the great Subjects of this Work, are allowed to surpass in Verdure and natural Beauty, whatever is to be found in those Countries [France and Italy].

The Situation on a Rising Ground is most courted, and has the greatest Advantages, provided it is not too steep, but the Slope easy and imperceptible, where one may enjoy a great deal of Level, and a good quantity of Water.

As to the Colour of Good Earth; it should be gray, inclining to black; the whitish Earths are never good.

What Advantage would it be, to plant a Garden in a Place that is buried, and has no kind of Prospect? . . . For my own part, I esteem nothing more diverting and agreeable in a Garden, than a fine View, and the Prospect of a noble Country.

The true size for a handsome Garden, may take in 30 or 40 acres, not more.

There should always be a Descent from the Building to the Garden, of three Steps at least: this renders the Fabrick [the house] more dry and wholsome.

A Parterre is the first Thing that should present itself to Sight, and possess the Ground next the Fabrick whether in Front, or on the Sides.

If there be no Vista . . . or some Village too near adjoining, the Houses of which make no agreeable Sight; you may then edge the Parterre with Pallisades [high hedges] and Groves, to hide those ill-favour'd Objects.

Groves make the Chief of a Garden.

Gardens on a perfect Level are certainly the best . . . [and] are less chargeable to keep than others.

The end of this Terrass is terminated by an Opening, which the French call a Claire-voie, or an Ah-ah, with a dry Ditch at the foot of it.

Yews and Shrubs on a Parterre, should never be permitted to grow above four or five Foot high at most.

Bramham Park, Yorkshire, was the only large formal garden left in England until the disastrous storm of 1962. This illustration, taken before the storm, shows the 'Four Faces', an urn placed at the junction of four alleys of beech hedges under beech trees.

A forest, John James says, consists of great trees very high, with 'Ridings cut for Hunting' through them, no hedges, no gravel. They should be planted in a star, with a large circle in the middle where the ridings meet. A coppice-wood should be cut to the ground every nine years. A wood is of the middle height, with a high hedge, and within the wood are spaces either hedged or trellised, possibly with fountains or some kind of arbour-work, and gravel. An 'Open Grove' is a series of squares, but with no trees in the middle. Alleys planted with lime or horse chestnut should have low hedges, 'three feet or breast high'. He recommends 'Woods of Ever-Greens' as being the finest of all.

Inkpen Old Rectory, Berkshire. A small garden planted in 1695, the only surviving small garden designed in the French manner, with alleys and 'patte d'oie' of yew, holly and beech.

Wrest Park. The French influence finally predominates. The Great Canal and Thomas Archer's Temple.

A narrow border should be four feet wide, five or six for a larger one. They should always be laid with a sharp rising in the middle, like 'an Ass's back ... being in no way agreeable to the Eye when they are flat'. 'Borders are made strait, circular or in Cants [by which he means in any way that avoids a right-angle at a corner] and are turned into Volutes, Scrolls, Knots, and other Compartiments.'

'Borders serve to bound and enclose Parterres, that they be not hurt by walking in them.' They were of earth or sand, sometimes gravel. They could be set out with flowers, shrubs and yews, the flowers planted in rows and squares, each separate from the other, the shrubs and yews clipped.

'When the Weeds are too big, you pluck them up by the Roots with your Hands, before you turn up the Ground, which is called *Weeding*.'

From The Theory and Practice of Gardening, *Done from the French Original, printed at Paris, Anno 1709, by John James of Greenwich, 1712:*

'You should observe, in placing and distributing the several Parts of a Garden, always to oppose them one to the other. For Example; A Wood to a Parterre, or a Bowling-Green; and not to put all the Parterres on one Side, and all the Wood on the other; nor to set a Bowling-Green against a Bason, which would be one Gap against another. This must be constantly avoided, by setting the Full against the Void, and Flat-works, against the Raised, to make a Contrariety ... For it would be very disagreeable to find the same Thing on both Sides ... This Fault was formerly very common; but is not so of late, every one being now convinced, that the greatest Beauty of Gardens is Variety.

There are divers Sorts of Parterres, which may be all reduced to these Four that follow; namely, Parterres of Embroidery, Parterres of Compartiment, Parterres after the English Manner, and Parterres of Cut-work. There are also Parterres of Water, but at present they are quite out of Use.

Parterres of Embroidery are so called, because the Box wherewith they are planted, imitates Embroidery upon the Ground. These are the finest and most magnificent of all, and are sometimes accompanied with Knots and Scrolls of Grass-work. Their Bottom should be sanded, the better to distinguish the Foliage and Flourish'd-work of the Embroidery, which is usually filled with Smiths-Dust, or Black Earth. [In a note he says: 'Dross, or Scales of Iron. Smiths-Dust is either the Scales beaten off at the Anvil, or Iron Filings.']

Parterres of Compartiment differ from those of Embroidery, in that the same Symmetry of Design is repeated, as well in respect of the Ends as of the Sides. These

In the same year that John James published his book, Joseph Addison, poet, essayist and man of letters, wrote in *The Spectator*:

Our British Gardeners . . . instead of humouring Nature, love to deviate from it as much as possible. Our Trees rise in Cones, Globes and Pyramids. We see the marks of the Scissars upon every Plant and Bush. I do not know whether I am singular in my opinion; but for my part, I would rather look upon a Tree, and all its Luxuriancy and Diffusion of Boughs and Branches, than when it is thus cut and trimm'd into a mathematical Figure, and cannot but fancy that an Orchard in Flower looks more delightful, than all the little Labyrinths of the most finished Parterre.

At the time, he was 'singular in his opinion', but he was not to be so for long. In 1714, Queen Anne died and was succeeded on the throne by her second cousin, King George I. He had no English and he had no Queen.

Parterres are made up of Scrolls and other Grass-works, Knots, and Borders for Flowers, with a little well-disposed Embroidery, which Mixture produces an Effect very agreeable to the Eye. The Ground of these should be very well made, and filled with Sand between the Leaves; the narrow Paths that separate the Compartiments, we usually distinguish with Tile-shards, or Brick-dust. [In a note, 'powdered Tile or Brick, mix'd with Lime, which makes excellent Mortar, and is used by the French in Works under Water.']

Parterres after the English Manner are the plainest and meanest of all. They should consist only of large Grass-plots all of a Piece, or cut but little, and be encompassed with a Border of Flowers, separated from the Grass-work by a Path of Two or Three Foot wide, laid smooth, and sanded over, to make the greater Distinction. We give it the Name of Parterre a l'Angloise, because we had the Manner of it first from England. [In a note, 'The French understand a Path raked over only, and not rolled, as 'tis generally translated, to comply with our Custom of Rolling, which is not so much used by the French, their Gravel rarely binding, as ours does.']

Parterres of Cut-work, tho' not so fashionable at present, are however not unworthy our Regard. They differ from the others, in that all the Parts which compose them should be cut with Symmetry, and that they admit neither of Grass nor Embroidery, but only Borders edged with Box, that serve to raise Flowers in; and by means of a Path of convenient Breadth that runs round each Piece, you may walk through the whole Parterre without hurting any Thing: All these Paths should be sanded.'

79

The entrance to Cirencester Park from the town shows the 'Broad' avenue, five miles in length. Pope called it 'an immense design'. It reflects what Switzer called 'Extended or Rural and Forest Gardening'. Lord Bathurst began planting, and what Pope called 'joining willing woods', in 1715.

St. Paul's, Walden Bury, Hertfordshire, begun by Edward Gilbert in 1720. This remains one of the few formal gardens in England today. Subsequent additions have been most tactfully handled.

27 and 28 (*Overleaf*) Hampton Court, Herefordshire. Paintings by Leonard Knyff, 1699.

29 and 30 Needlework
Hangings from Stoke Edith,
Herefordshire, started about
1710.

31 and 32 Scenes near Cheltenham. Unknown Artist, about 1700.

Political power passed into the hands of the Prime Minister and the Court ceased to be the centre of social life. The nobility and gentry spent more time in the country.

At Cirencester Park, a huge forest was planted with ten avenues radiating from a star, a village church the visual point at the end of each; the great main avenue was centred on the Parish Church of Cirencester. At St. Paul's, Walden Bury, an arm of the goose-foot led the eye to the local church. At Studley Royal, the main approach to the house was centred on Ripon Cathedral.

But the way ahead was pointed by Sir John Vanbrugh, playwright and architect of Blenheim Palace, who, in 1715, built a mock castle on a hill at Claremont near Esher, not at all unlike the castle he built as his own house near Blackheath.

One of the first gardens of this time which we can regard, in the words of the first Queen Elizabeth, as 'mere English', is at Studley Royal in Yorkshire. It was begun around 1715 by John Aislabie, an ex-Chancellor who found it convenient to leave London. He had married the

Stephen Switzer's plan of Paston Manor, from his *Nobleman, Gentleman and Gardener's Recreation* of 1718. Here the great formal gardens and main avenue, reminiscent of Wise's plan for Blenheim, are surrounded by a series of formal and semi-formal patterns through the surrounding woodland.

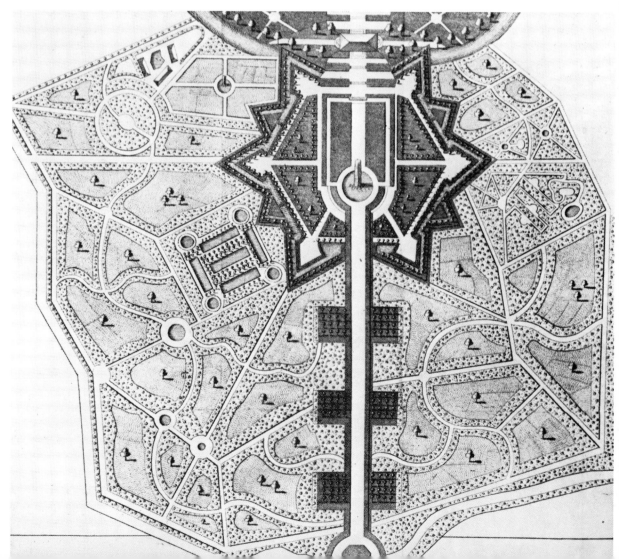

widowed daughter-in-law of Edmund Waller, and must therefore have known the garden at Hall Barn.

He dammed a natural stream in a natural valley. The stream was made into a straight canal and on either side were placed, asymmetrically, formal ponds, circular and half-moon shaped. The floor of the valley was raised and levelled just enough to contain the water. The natural hillsides were planted with native trees, and sycamore. A clipped yew hedge divided the trees from the grass. Where banks were required, they were formal in shape, that is to say they were made with corners, or ramped.

It was, in a sense, a parterre of water, said by John James to be 'quite out of Use', by which he meant out of fashion. The Spirit of the Place, in the old Druid tradition, was most tactfully consulted, though the one original temple building was of undoubted Roman ancestry.

It was a unique garden always and we must be deeply grateful that it is still there for us to see today.

Opposite, above and below:
Studley Royal in Yorkshire. The English genius for garden design here asserts itself for the first time. There is little trace of France here and none of Holland. John Aislabie, a discredited Chancellor of the Exchequer, implicated in the 'South Sea Bubble', began his garden here in 1715, after his release from the Tower of London. This is an early example—Stourhead is another—of the garden being completely divorced from the house.

Garden Gate at Hall Barn.

PART THREE

A Temple in the Grove,
1725-1755

Kent's design for the Vale of Venus at Rousham about 1739.

Hurstbourne Priors. An elaborate cascade at the head of a canal, with a castellated folly behind, designed by Thomas Archer about 1712.

An elaborate water garden begun in 1718 at Ebberston Hall by William Thompson. Ebberston Hall itself is hardly more than a glorified pavilion.

As Mighty as the Spade

'Not far from Lewis, I saw an Ancient Lady, and a Lady of very good Quality, I assure you, drawn to Church in her Coach with Six Oxen; nor was it done in Frolick or Humour, but sheer Necessity, the Way being so stiff and deep, that no Horses could go in it.'

The exact date of this incident, recorded by Daniel Defoe in his *Tour of England and Wales*, is not known, but it was probably within the first fifteen years of the eighteenth century. Elsewhere, he said:

Upon the top of that Mountain begins a vast extended Moor or Waste, which, for fifteen or sixteen Miles together due North, presents you with neither Hedge, House or Tree, but a waste and houling Wilderness, over which when Strangers travel, they are obliged to take Guides, or it would be next to impossible not to lose their way.

Nothing can be more surprising of its Kind, than for a Stranger coming from the North, suppose from Sheffield in Yorkshire, for that is the first Town of Note, and wandering or labouring to pass this difficult Desart Country, and seeing no End of it, and almost

Vanbrugh's Castle Howard, showing the original 'architectural' garden layout. The 'wilderness or wood within the walls', with its maze-like appearance, existed until the middle of the 18th century.

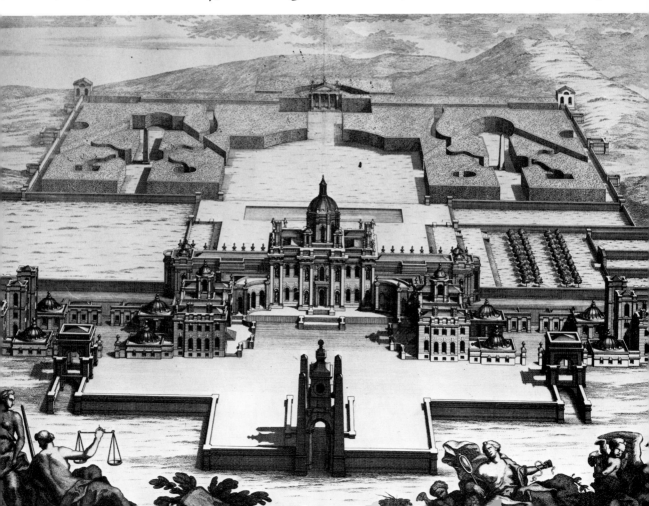

Thomas Duncombe laid out the great terrace at Duncombe with Vanbrugh's help in 1712. *Left*: the statue, at the end of what was a parterre in front of the house, stands in the middle of the terrace, which has a temple at either end of it. *Right*: the wall, dividing the garden from the park, represents a half-way stage between the bastion type wall and the sunk fence, or HaHa, that was to change the English garden.

> discouraged and beaten out with the Fatigue of it, (just such was our case) on a sudden the Guide brings him to this Precipice, where he looks down from a frightful heighth, and a comfortless, barren, and, as he thought endless Moor, into the most delightful Valley, with the most pleasant Garden, and most beautiful Palace in the World.

This was Defoe's first view of Chatsworth. The countryside was still quite distinct from the parks and gardens which surrounded the houses. In the middle years of the eighteenth century this was to be changed entirely. The park, simplified and expanded, was to merge visually with the countryside which, 'improved', was to merge visually with the park.

The system of agriculture which had been followed until this time was the open field or strip system, whereby one man farmed a series of 'strips' which could be at some distance from each other. It was extremely wasteful in terms of labour, and the system of enclosures which started at this time resulted in larger fields, all devoted to one crop only.

They had, in general, a natural division—a stream, a wood, an existing road—and were not laid out like a chessboard; they followed the contours of the land.

88

33 and 34 Scenes near Cheltenham. Unknown Artist, about 1700.

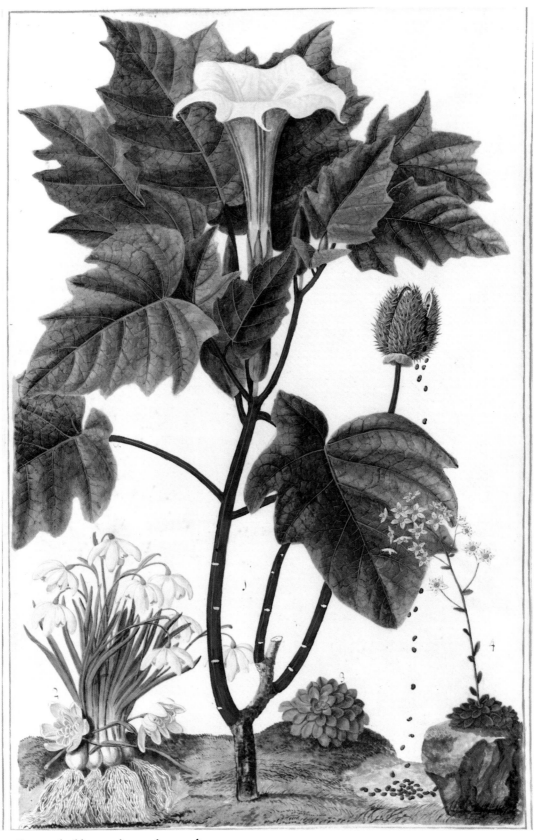

35 Datura, double snowdrop and two sedums.

From: The Duchess of Beaufort's Book, 1703.

36 A nerine in a pot.

37 A pelargonium.

38 A guava tree.

39 An Indian hibiscus.

40–44 Garden at Hartwell House, laid out about 1690. Paintings by Balthasar Nebot, 1738.

46 The China Orange. Unknown Artist.

45 The Pineapple. From a painting by G. D. Ehret.

47 *Right*
  'The yellow martagon lily, the double Persian
  ranunculus, the Pyrenean Houndstongue and
  the round-leaved Judas Tree.' Painting by
  Thomas Robins the Younger, 1784.

48 Elecampane.

49 Jerusalem Artichoke.

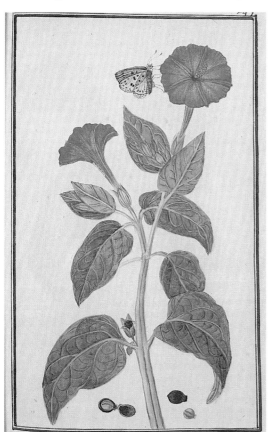

50 Marvel of Peru.

51 Monkshood.

Garden Flowers of the 1730s.

52 Dunham Massey, painted by John Harris, about 1750.

53 (*Left*) and 54 (*Right*) Claremont. Unknown Artist, after 1729.

Left and right: Castle Howard: The obelisk commemorating the Duke of Marlborough erected in 1714. The Kitchen Garden begun in 1703.

It required an act of Parliament to enclose land in this way and more than three hundred were passed in the course of the century. Two and a half million acres of open fields and two million acres of common land were brought into intensive cultivation. The yield of food much more than doubled, sheep produced twice as much meat and three times as much wool in value. The agricultural countryside, as we know it today, was the lasting result.

The device which separated the park from the countryside was known as the sunk fence, or fosse. A trench was dug and a retaining wall built on one side of it; the other side was made into a gradual slope, up to the original level of the ground. From a distance, the fields appeared as a simple continuation of the park; but the sheep and cows could not get into it.

It has become known to us as a HaHa, perhaps because those who observed it said 'Aha', while those who did not caused their friends to say 'Haha' when they fell into it. Horace Walpole, son of the first Prime Minister, said that the common people called them Ha!Ha's! 'to express their surprise at finding a sudden and unperceived check to their walk'. They could be straight or curved, made of brick or stone, more rarely of stakes driven together into the ground. In hilly country, a wall could be built and then back-filled with earth up to its top. There are still many to be seen in England.

Castle Howard: Vanbrugh's romantic park wall, with its crenellated bastions, was built around 1725.

Castle Howard: The grass walk to the Temple of the Four Winds from the south front of Lord Carlisle's great palace. The walk following an old lane to the village (which was demolished to make way for the house) was conceived c. 1725, making it one of the earliest 'natural' landscapes.

90

Castle Howard: the Temple of the Four Winds with Hawksmoor's vast mausoleum in the background. Vanbrugh designed the temple in 1726.

The great landscape designer credited by Horace Walpole with the idea of the HaHa was Charles Bridgeman. He had worked with John Vanbrugh and Henry Wise while they were making the original garden at Blenheim early in the century and he rose to be Royal Gardener to King George II. 'Bridgeman', wrote Horace Walpole, 'banished verdant sculpture, and did not even revert to the square precision of the foregoing age. He enlarged his plans, disdained to make every division tally to its opposite; and though he still adhered much to straight walks with high clipped hedges, they were only his great lines; the rest he diversified by wilderness, and with loose groves of oak, though still within surrounding hedges. . . . In the royal garden at Richmond [he] dared to introduce cultivated fields, and even morsels of a forest appearance, by the sides of those endless and tiresome walks, that stretched out of one into another without intermission.'

Bridgeman's work hardly survived the next generation but, fortunately for us, some excellent paintings of his garden at Claremont still exist. His amphitheatre there has recently been restored.

While economics could have played their part in the desire for simplicity—the turf at Canons, in Middlesex, was, in 1721, scythed twice or three times a week and it was weeded every day—the poets and writers of the day also played an important part. Chief among these was

Alexander Pope. In the garden that he made for himself at Twickenham, there was a grotto, a shell temple, a large mount, a grove, a bowling green, two small mounts, an obelisk in memory of his mother, a stove, a vineyard, an orangery and a garden house. There was a series of linked grass walks, not unlike the 'patte d'oie', but they were now carved through woods, instead of being accompanied by two lines of trees.

John James had said that it was 'the great Business of an Architect . . . with his utmost Art and good Œconomy to improve the natural Advantages, and to redress the Imperfections, Shelvings, and inequalities of the Ground. With these Precautions he should guide and restrain the Impetuosity of his Genius, never swerving from Reason, but constantly submitting, and conforming himself to that which suits best with the natural Situation of the Place.' Now, in 1731, Pope was to write: 'Consult the genius of the place in all.' The difference here was that, while James did not disdain the appearance of Art, as later writers were to call it—that is to say the use of alleys, avenues, rows of trees and clipped hedges—Pope's idea was that everything should look natural.

In his *Essay on Criticism*, 1715, he said:

First follow Nature, and your judgment frame
By her just standard, which is still the same:
Unerring Nature, still divinely bright,
One clear, unchang'd, and universal light,
Life, force, and beauty, must to all impart,
At once the source, and end, and test of Art.
That Art is best which most resembles her,
And still presides, yet never does appear.

These words, though addressed to young poets, were nevertheless entirely relevant to the landscaping practice of the time. The problem was, simply, to decide what was meant by 'Nature'. The eighteenth century, as it progressed, changed its opinions about this; but one thing was certain. Anything clipped, anything straight, anything with regular angles, was not natural, was therefore to be deplored and was, in most cases, to be destroyed.

Ichnographica Rustica, or, the Nobleman, Gentleman, and Gardener's Recreation by Stephen Switzer, 'Seedsman and Gardener at the Seedshop at Westminster Hall' was first published in 1718. A second edition, in 1742, bore the words:

'With above Fifty Copper Plates, done by the best Hands, which, though first published above twenty years ago, has given rise to every thing of the kind, which has been done since.'

Although Switzer's work suffered the same fate as Bridgeman's, there is no reason to suppose that the advice contained in his volumes was not widely followed. It was practical and extremely detailed.

The New Principles of Gardening *by Batty Langley of Twickenham were published in 1728.*

He offers practical advice on how to lay out a garden, but his shapes are all geometrical. He suggests the following shrubs for the Wilderness. The names in italic are the present botanical names.

Spanish Broom	*Genista hispanica*
Laburnum	
Tulip Tree	
Senna	*Colutea arborescens*
Arbor Judae	*Cercis siliquastrum*
Mezerion	*Daphne mezereum*
Jessamine	

'Unless with Poles you fix it to the Wall,
Its own deceitful Trunk will quickly fall.'

Honeysuckle	
Lilac	
Pomegranate	

'Tis a hardy Plant, and will endure the Winter Frosts, cold Winds, &c.'

Althaea Frutex	*Hibiscus syriacus*
Syringa	*Philadelphus*
Guilder-Rose	*Viburnum opulus*
Almond	
Mirabalon Plumb	*Prunus cerasifera*
Double-blossomed Cherry	*Prunus avium plena*
Furze-Bush and English Broom	

'Were they not common, they would be valued, and cultivated with as much Eagerness as any Ever-green or Shrub whatsoever.'

Maracoc	*Passiflora caerulea*
The Cinamon Rose	*Rosa cinnamomea*
The Damask Rose	probably *Rosa damascena bifera*
The Cabbage Rose	*Rosa centifolia*
Rosa Mundi	*Rosa gallica versicolor*
White Musk	*Rosa moschata*
Red Rose	*Rosa gallica maxima*
Yellow Rose	*Rosa spinossissima*
Sweet Briar	probably *Rosa eglanteria*, perhaps *rubiginosa*

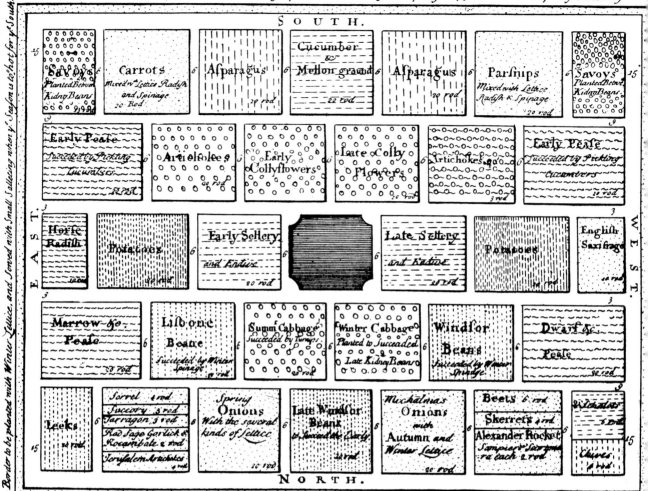

Batty Langley was known also for his architectural pattern books, which gave detailed instructions, with innumerable plans, for laying out gardens. This example shows a layout for a kitchen garden.

He suggests that flowers should be 'the Inhabitants of the inward Parts of an open Wilderness, &c. planted promiscuously in the Quarters thereof; but not in regular Lines, as has been the common Way. But, on the contrary, in little Thickets, or Clusters, seemingly without any other Order than what Nature directed, which, of all others, is the most beautiful.'

He went on: 'N.B. That in the Disposition of these Clusters of Flowers, Care must be taken to mix the several Sorts in such a Manner, as for every Part to be equally adorn'd throughout the whole Year.'

The list of plants that he offers differs very little from that of John Parkinson a hundred years before; if anything, it is rather shorter.

He says, for instance, that designs in 'Clipt Plants, Flowers, and other trifling Decorations [are] fit only for little Town-gardens, and not for the expansive Tracts of the Country', nevertheless '[I would not] be understood to condemn all Enclosed and Flower-Gardens, since they are absolutely necessary in Cities, Towns and other bounded places.' He does not entirely disapprove time spent 'observing the colour of a tulip'. We may suppose that gardens of this kind continued to be made in and around the towns long after they had been forgotten in the country.

He advises his readers to pay their gardeners properly and to spend an annual sum on their gardens, accomplishing all changes gradually. 'The Kitchen Garden, Fish Ponds &c about a Seat, are not only a great Ornament, but will make a great Abatement in the Expenses of House-keeping.'

He is opposed to extravagance and he is opposed to Charles Bridgeman.

The same extravagant way of thinking prevailed also to a great degree, in that otherwise ingenious Designer, in his Plan of Lakes and Pieces of Water, without any regard to the Goodness of the Land, which was to be overflowed. But which he generally designed so large, as to make a whole Country look like an Ocean.

The whole Art of Designing consists in a just Agreement of the several Parts one with another; and the adapting of the whole to the Nature and Uses of the Place, for which your Design is formed.

> Villa's and Gardens you will best Command,
> If timely you engage a Master's Hand,
> Whose artful Pencil shall on Paper trace
> The whole Design, and figure out the Place.

He has sections on woods, groves, wildernesses and parks.

. . . endeavour to follow and improve the Advantages of Nature, and not to strain her beyond her due Bounds. . . . It would be a fault to level all those little Eminencies and pleasing labyrinths of Nature. . . . Wood is misplaced, when it is too near the Eye in any Place, when it comes so close up to it, as to admit of no open Lawn or Breathing . . . it likewise thickens the Air, and makes the Situation unhealthy.

95

Then, to one's great surprise, he offers 'A Plann of some Groves in Quincunx &c with two Mazes and Labyrinths'. He writes 'On Hopyards and their Management, A Curious Dissertation on Mushrooms, On the Choice of Situations, & Soil, On Winter-fallowing, Of the Nature of Dung, Of Superficial Dressings by Coal Ashes, and by Sea Sand, Of Ploughing, Of Sowing, Of Draining of Lands.'

The great development in the large gardens of this time was to be the Belt Walk, or Ribbon Walk, an informal succession of paths both of grass and gravel, leading through a variety of scenes, some natural and some contrived, very often starting at the house and returning to it.

'This Anfilade or Circuit', wrote Switzer, 'ought to be Six or Seven Yards wide at least.' He advises placing clumps of trees and buildings on 'eminencies', suggests that 'all the adjacent country be laid open to View' and says it is certain that 'no Nation in the World is bless'd with more natural Conveniences than we are'. Gardening, he says, 'is easy, quiet, and such as puts neither the Body nor Mind into those violent Agitations or precipitate and imminent Dangers that many other Exercises (in themselves very warrantable) do'.

A Natural Reaction

Horace Walpole's *Essay on Modern Gardening* was not published until 1785, but the gardens he wrote about were all made at this time. He entirely dismisses the previous style, mentions that 'at Lady Orford's at Piddletown in Dorsetshire, there was a double enclosure of thirteen gardens, each I suppose not much above an hundred yards square. . . . A bowling green was all the lawn admitted in those times, a circular lake the extent of magnificence.' At Marshal Biron's garden, in Paris, which consisted of fourteen acres, 'there were nine thousand pots of asters'. He quotes Sir William Temple, who had laid out a notable garden in Surrey at the end of the previous century, as saying that irregular gardening was extremely difficult; 'whereas in regular figures it is hard to make any great and remarkable faults'.

'Fortunately', said Horace Walpole, 'Kent and a few others were not so timid, or we might still be going up and down stairs in the open air.'

55 Arcadian Landscape
by Claude, 1675.

56 Arcadian Landscape
by l'Orizonte, about 1725.

57, 58, 59 Chiswick House. Paintings by Pieter Rysbrack, about 1730.

60 Stowe.

61

62

63

64

65

66

61–66 Stowe.

Kent's design for Gates at Euston in Suffolk, showing the planting of clumps of trees.

William Kent was born at Bridlington, into a family of which little is known, and was trained as a sign painter. He made his own way to Rome where, in 1716, he met a number of English noblemen making the Grand Tour of Europe, at that time an indispensable part of their education. Among them was the Earl of Burlington, who remained his patron for the rest of his life. He worked as an architect, an interior decorator, a furniture designer and a landscape designer, with considerable success in each field.

It was in Rome that Kent, and the travelling noblemen, encountered the paintings of Salvator Rosa, Gaspard Poussin and Claude Lorrain. They were paintings from the end of the previous century; Salvator Rosa died in 1673, Poussin in 1675 and Claude in 1682. They were idealised landscape paintings, softened or darkened, of hills and valleys, great clouds, splendid trees, very often groups of people and, invariably, buildings or groups of buildings, nearly always of classical ancestry. If the idea grew that this kind of landscape could be re-created in England, one should also remember that both Kent and the noblemen had seen the actual landscape of Italy.

In the words of Horace Walpole:

At that moment appeared Kent, painter enough to taste the charms of landscape, bold and opionated enough to dare and to dictate. He leaped the fence and saw that all nature was a garden. He felt the delicious contrast of hill and valley changing imperceptibly into each other, tasted the beauty of the gentle swell, or concave scoop, and remarked how loose groves crowned an easy eminence with happy ornament.

Where objects were wanting to animate his horizon, his taste as an architect could bestow termination. His buildings, his seats, his temples, were more the work of his pencil than his compasses.

But of all the beauties that he added to the face of this beautiful country, none surpassed his management of water. Adieu to canals, circular basons and cascades tumbling down marble steps, the last absurd magnificence of Italian and French villas. . . . The gentle stream was taught to serpentise seemingly at its pleasure . . . . Its borders were smoothed, but preserved their waving irregularity. A few trees scattered here and there on its edges. . . . Thus dealing in none but the colours of nature, and catching its most favourable features, men saw a new creation opening before their eyes. The living landscape was chastened and polished, not transformed.

Stowe: Bridgeman's central axis from the original south entry to the garden between Vanbrugh's lakeside pavilions. The house lies behind the fountain, which is in the middle of the octagonal lake.

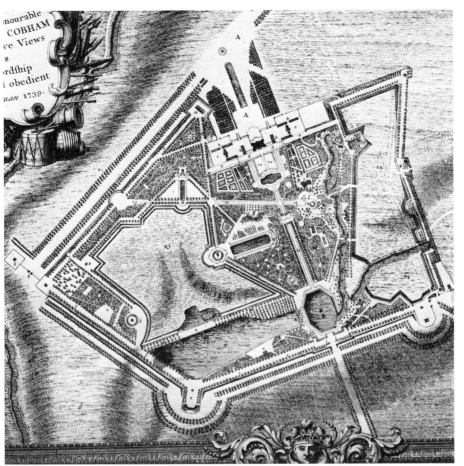

Two plans showing the 'naturalising' of the formal layout at Stowe, Lord Cobham's great garden, where Vanbrugh, Bridgeman, Kent and Brown all contributed to the design

Left: Sarah Bridgeman's plan of 1739 still showing, at that date, her husband's plan for the garden of about twenty years earlier. Charles Bridgeman first started to work at Stowe in 1713.

Below: A plan of 1797 shows the lake 'naturalised' and the Elysian Fields, to the right of the house, which were landscaped by William Kent after 1733.

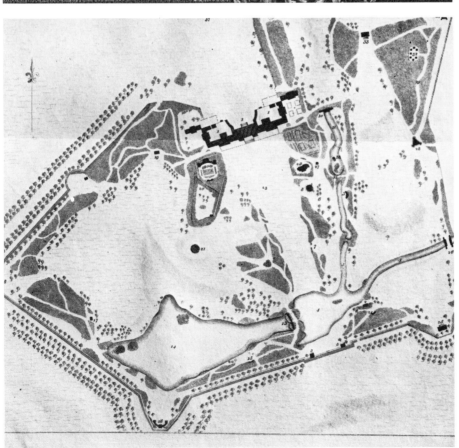

The interest in landscaping, as opposed to horticulture, was now widely spread. Here is a description of an evening dress made in 1740. Mrs. Delany, who wrote about it, invented a kind of paper mosaic for representing flowers:

'. . . Delany forms her mimic bowers
Her paper foliage, and her silken flowers.'

She corresponded with Swift and introduced Fanny Burney to the Court. The dress concerned was worn at a Court held by Frederick, Prince of Wales, father of King George III.

'The Duchess of Queensbury's clothes pleased me best; they were white satin embroidered, the bottom of the petticoat *brown hills* covered with all sorts of weeds, and *every breadth* had *an old stump of a tree* that run almost to the top of the petticoat, broken and ragged and worked with brown chenille, round which twined nasturtians, ivy, honeysuckles, periwinkles, convolvuluses and all sorts of twining flowers which spread and covered the petticoat, vines with leaves variegated as you have seen them by the sun, all rather smaller than nature, which made them look very light; the robings and facings were little green banks with all sorts of weeds, and the sleeves and the rest of the gown loose twining branches of the same sort as those on the petticoat; many of the leaves were finished with gold, and part of the stumps of the trees looked like gilding of the sun. I never saw a piece of work so prettily fancied, and am quite angry with myself for not having the same thought, for it is infinitely handsomer than mine, and could *not* cost *much more*.'

In 1748, she offered this description of Lord Orrery's garden, actually made near Dublin, but very much in the English mode:

'Nothing is completed yet but an *hermitage*, which is about an acre of ground—an island, planted with all variety of trees, shrubs, and flowers that will grow in this country, abundance of little winding walks, differently embellished with little seats and banks; in the midst is placed an hermit's cell, made of the roots of trees, the floor is paved with pebbles, there is a couch made of matting, and little wooden stools, a table with a manuscript on it, a pair of spectacles, a leathern bottle; and hung up in different parts, an hourglass, a weatherglass and several mathematical instruments, a shelf of books, another of wooden platters and bowls, another of earthen ones, in short everything that you might imagine necessary for a recluse. *Four little gardens surround his house*—an orchard, a flower-garden, a physick-garden, and a kitchen garden, with a kitchen to boil a teakettle or so: I never saw so pretty *a whim* so *thoroughly well* executed.'

Later, Thomas Whately's comment was to be:

'A hermitage is the habitation of a recluse; it should be distinguished by its solitude, and its simplicity; but if it is filled with crucifixes, hour-glasses, beads, and every other trinket which can be thought of, the attention is diverted from enjoying the retreat to examining the particulars.'

Objects 'to animate the horizon' now became the rage. As early as 1683, John Vanbrugh had been sent to France to study the arts. He built the castle at Claremont in 1715, and by 1720 was at work at Castle Howard and at Duncombe Park, both in Yorkshire. At the former, he built the Temple of the Four Winds in an angle of the HaHa, which was reached from the house by a gradually ascending terrace. At Duncombe Park, a circular temple stood at each end of a levelled grass walk, which followed a contour of the hill. The house, with a flat parterre in front of it, stood more or less at the centre of the walk; and the two temples could not be seen from one another. Groves of trees separated them and a particularly magnificent HaHa retained the hill at another point. All this can be seen today.

Kent's plan of Rousham of 1737. The garden remains today almost as Kent planned it.

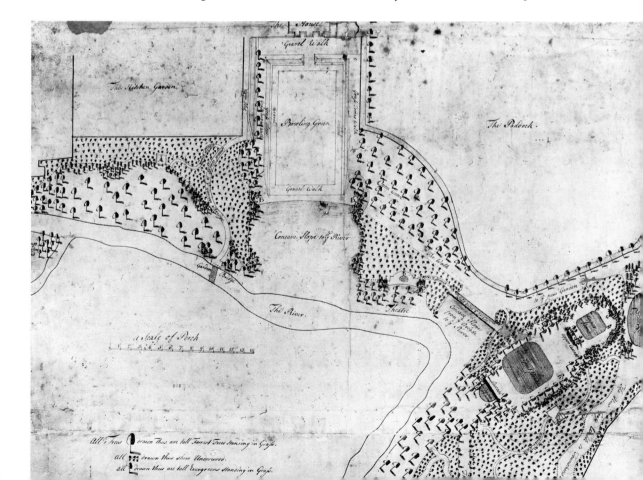

At Stowe, in Buckinghamshire, and at Rousham, in Oxfordshire, Kent followed Bridgeman. The garden at Rousham is the more complete of the two, as no one followed Kent. It is made on the north slope of a hill, facing, at the best, the north-east, and has a certain sombre quality for this reason. But it slopes to the river Cherwell, whose shape Kent did not attempt to alter. The previous generation would, perhaps, have made it into a series of canals; the one which followed would probably have turned it into a lake.

Rousham: Kent's drawing of the mill—a Gothick folly attached to a cottage—and the 'eyecatcher', placed outside the garden proper to lead the eye into the surrounding countryside.

[Kent] was neither without assistance nor faults [concluded Horace Walpole]. Mr. Pope undoubtedly contributed to form his taste. . . . I do not know whether the disposition of the garden at Rousham, laid out for general Dormer, and in my opinion the most engaging of all Kent's works, was not planned on the model of Mr. Pope's. . . . His clumps were puny; he aimed at immediate effect, and planted not for futurity. . . . His ruling principle was that 'nature abhors a straight line'. His mimics, for every genius has his apes, seemed to think that he could love nothing but what was crooked.

It was to be a guiding principle for many years.

102

Rousham: A garden
seat designed by Kent.

Rousham: Kent's
winding rill, octagon
pool plus cold bath.
The rill leads one
through a woodland
walk.

Yon stream that wanders down the dale,
The spiral wood, the winding vale,
The path which, wrought with hidden skill,
Slow twining scales yon distant hill
With fir invested—all combine
To recommend the waving line.

William Shenstone

The 'Praeneste' at Rousham, placed to give a view over the Cherwell below to the surrounding countryside.

Four very influential gardens from this time were made by their owners, without professional advice. Stourhead, in Wiltshire, was inherited by Henry Hoare from his father in 1741; and the poet, William Shenstone, began work on his estate, The Leasowes near Halesowen, now a golf club, in 1743. In 1735 in Surrey, near Weybridge, Philip Southcote bought Woburn Farm, which has entirely disappeared; and, at Pains Hill, also in Surrey, the Hon. Charles Hamilton began to alter his estate at about the same time. The outline of his garden can still be discerned today.

All were made on the principle of the circuit walk, Stourhead differing from the others in that the circuit was simply round a lake, created for the purpose. At Pains Hill, the walk followed a lake, made above the River Mole and fed by a huge water-wheel from it, and then left it, an important incident in the walk but not its focus.

Left: Chinese Bridge at Pains Hill, Surrey.

Right: Gothick tent at Pains Hill.

Fortunately for us, two of these were visited by Horace Walpole and three of them by Thomas Whately, while they were at their best and under the supervision of their owners. Mr. Whately was a Secretary of State under Lord North and, by 1771, his *Observations on Modern Gardening* had reached its third edition. (He never refers to a HaHa. It is always a sunk fence.)

Of Woburn Farm, he wrote:

The place contains an hundred and fifty acres, of which near five and thirty are adorned to the highest degree.

A path generally of sand or gravel, is conducted in a waving line, sometimes close under the hedge, sometimes at a little distance from it; and the turf on either side is diversified with little groupes of shrubs, of firs, or the smallest trees, and often with beds of flowers; these are rather too profusely strewed, and hurt the eye by their littlenesses; but then they replenish the air with their perfumes, and every gale is full of fragrancy.

This walk is properly garden; all within it is farm; the whole lies on two sides of a hill, and on a flat at the foot of it; the flat is divided into corn-fields; the pastures occupy the hill; they are surrounded by the walk.

These hedges are sometimes thickened with flowering shrubs; and in every corner, or vacant space, is a rosary, a close or an open clump, or a bed of flowers: but if the parterre has been rifled for the embellishment of the fields, the country has on the other hand been searched for plants new in a garden; and the shrubs and flowers which used to be deemed peculiar to the one, have been liberally transferred to the other. . . . A more moderate use of them would, however, have been better, and the variety more pleasing, had it been less licentious.

But the excess is only in the borders of the walk; the scenes through which it leads are truly elegant, every where rich, and always agreeable. A peculiar chearfulness overspreads [it].

The lowings of the herds, the bleating of the sheep, and the tinklings of the bell-wether, resound through the plantation; even the clucking of poultry is not omitted; for a menagerie of very simple design is placed near the Gothic building; a small serpentine river is provided for the water-fowl; while the others stray among the flowering shrubs on the banks, or straggle about the neighbouring lawn.

This kind of landscape garden was known as a Ferme Ornée, literally an ornamented farm, and some were more ornamented than others. As Thomas Whately observed, The Leasowes presented a perfect picture of Shenstone's mind, simple, elegant and amiable.

A walk as unaffected and unadorned as a common field path, is conducted through several enclosures.

Near the entrance into the grounds, this walk plunges suddenly into a dark narrow dell, filled with small trees which grow upon abrupt, and broken steeps, and watered by a brook, which falls among roots and stones down a natural cascade into the hollow. . . . The end of this sequestered spot opens to a pretty landskip, which is very simple; for the parts are but few, and all the objects are familiar; they are only the piece of water, some fields on an easy ascent beyond it, and the steeple of the church above them.

A *Ferme Ornée*-ornamental farm buildings, in this case castellated.

The next scene is more solitary; it is confined within itself, a rude neglected bottom, the sides of which are over-run with bushes and fern, interspersed with several trees. A rill runs also through this little valley . . . the stream winds through the wood in a succession of cascades . . . alders and hornbean grow in the midst of its bed . . . beyond them is a slight coppice, just sufficient to skreen the spot from open view; but it casts no gloom. . . . The walk . . . over-looks not only the little wild below, but some cornfields on the opposite side, which by their chearfulness and proximity dissipate every idea of solitude.

The variety of The Leasowes is wonderful; all the enclosures are totally different. . . . The lower field comprehends both sides of a deep dip; the upper is one large knole; the former is encompassed with a thick wood; the latter is open; a slight hedge, and a serpentine river, are all its boundary. Several trees, single or in groups, are scattered over the swells of the ground; not a tree is to be seen on all the steeps of the hollow.

From the knole . . . the beautiful farm of The Leasowes is included in the landskip. In other spots, plantations have been raised, or openings cut, on purpose to shut out, or let in . . . certain points of view.

The path is conducted along the bank to the foot of a hill, which it climbs in an aukward zig-zag; and on the top it enters a straight walk . . . too artificial for the character of The Leasowes.

Even the hedges are distinguished from each other; a common quickset fence is in one place the separation; in another, it is a lofty hedge-row, thick from the top to the bottom; in a third, it is a continued range of trees, with all their stems clear.

The inscriptions which abound in the place are another striking peculiarity; they are well-known and justly admired; and the elegance of the poetry, and the aptness of the quotations, atone for their length and their number; but in general, inscriptions please no more than once.

An urn in a lonely grove, or in the midst of a field, is a favourite embellishment at The Leasowes.

The buildings are mostly mere seats, or little root-houses; a ruin of a priory is the largest, and that has no particular beauty to commend it.

The objects are borrowed partly from the scenes which this country exhibited some centuries ago, and partly from Arcadia; the priory, and a Gothic seat, still more particularly characterised by an inscription in obsolete language and the black letter, belong to the one; the urns, Virgil's obelisk, and a rustic temple of Pan, to the other.

The Classick, the Gothick and the Rustick

The first deliberately built ruin is thought to have been made at Hagley, in Worcestershire, in 1745. It was principally a round castellated tower and had, said Horace Walpole, 'the true rust of the Baron's Wars'. It was shortly followed by a Temple of Theseus, in the Greek manner, and these were two of the 'incidents' that occurred in the course of a twelve and a half mile circuit. There was an octagon seat dedicated to James Thomson the poet, erected in his favourite place, and 'a solitary urn, chosen by Mr. Pope for the spot', a rotunda on a knoll, a hermitage composed of roots and moss, and a view from a bridge, described by Thomas Whately as 'a perfect opera scene'.

erson Miller's design for the Gothick 'ruin' in the park
impole, 1750.

The Gothick 'ruin' in the park at Hagley.

109

Alfred's Hall in the park at Cirencester, one of the first castellated follies to be built, about 1725. Etching by Thomas Robins, 1763.

There was a degree of make-believe in all this, the creation of a mood, the re-creation of a landscape from abroad; but in general the character of the English landscape was strong enough to embrace even the most eccentric structures—the most eccentric were called follies—and to include them.

At Stourhead, the original buildings were the Pantheon and the Temple of Flora, which were classical, and the Grotto, which had a practical function; 'the most fortunately placed grotto is that at Stourhead', wrote Horace Walpole, 'where the river bursts from the urn of its god, and passes on its course through the cave'. The lake at Stourhead was made by damming two streams and linking a series of fishponds. The banks were originally planted with beech and larch, under-planted with cherry laurel.

Exterior of the Hermit's Park House at Badminton. On the seat outside is written: 'Here loungers loiter. Here the weary rest'.

Interior of the Hermit's Park House at Badminton, probably designed by Thomas Wright in 1750.

Merlin's Cave and the Hermitage, in the grounds of Richmond Palace, designed by
William Kent for Queen Caroline, later destroyed by Brown.

67–74 (*and overleaf*) F. Nicholson's Views of Stourhead, 1813–14.

View of Badminton,
Canaletto, about 1748.

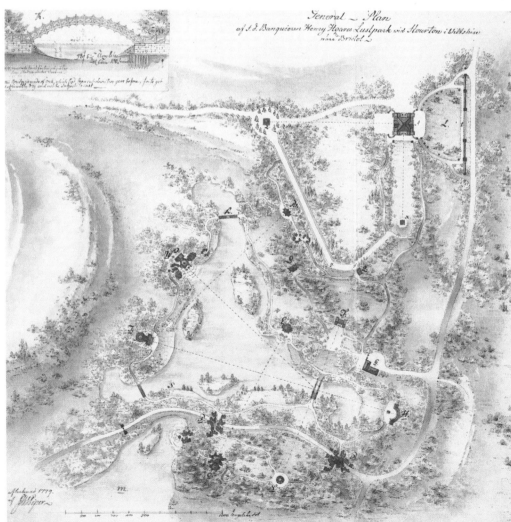

Plan of Stourhead,
F. M. Piper, 1779.

77 Crown Imperial.

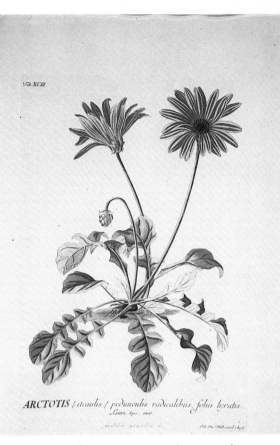

78 Arctotis acaulis. From a painting by G. D. Ehret.

79 Peony, from Lord Bute's collection.

80 'The West Indian Red Lily', a hippeastrum.

Flowers from the mid-eighteenth century.

At Pains Hill, said Horace Walpole, all was 'great and foreign and rude'; Thomas Whately found three bridges, a ruined arch, a grotto, a Gothic building and a hermit's cell: 'the design is as simple as the materials; and the furniture within is old and uncouth.' He describes a broad walk along the banks of the river, bordered with shrubs and flowers; but his most surprising information is contained in his description of the immediate surroundings to the house.

The spot is laid out in an elegant garden taste, pretending to be no more than pleasant. In the midst of the thicket which separates it from the park, is a parterre, and an orangerie, where the exotic plants are, during the summer, intermixed with common shrubs, and a constant succession of flowers. The space before the house is full of ornament; the ground is prettily varied; and several sorts of beautiful trees are disposed on the sides in little open plantations.

'Art' still survived near the house, though it was not to do so for much longer. The Circuit Garden was composed mainly of wood and water,

The garden of Goldney House at Clifton, where a Bristol merchant created a garden in only a few acres. The terrace, with its Gothick summerhouse, commanded a view of the port of Bristol in the valley below.

Goldney: Walls and
bastions supported the
terraces above and
divided the garden
proper from the
surrounding fields and
orchards.

grass and gravel, with buildings at intervals; and it was this kind of garden which was to be copied in other countries and known as the English Garden. It was adaptable, receptive to peculiar ornament and, most important of all, it could be of any size.

> Smooth, simple path! whose undulating line
> With sidelong tufts of flowery fragrance crown'd,
> Plain in its neatness spans my garden round;
> What, though two acres thy brief course confine.

Thus the Reverend William Mason in ecstatic mood; but the last word rests with Horace Walpole.

> Men tire of expence that is obvious to few spectators. . . . The Doric portico, the Palladian Bridge, the Gothic Ruin, the Chinese Pagoda, that surprise the stranger, soon lose their charms to their surfeited master. The lake that floats the valley is still more lifeless, and its lord seldom enjoys his expence but when he shows it to a visitor. But the ornament whose merit soonest fades, is the hermitage, or scene adapted to contemplation. It is almost comic to set aside a quarter of one's garden to be melancholy in. Prospect, animated prospect, is the theatre that will always be the most frequented.

It was to be the principal quest of the succeeding generation.

The entrance to the grotto at Goldney.

Goldney: The interior of the grotto. A stone river god presides at the head of a cascade. The owner's daughters encrusted much of the interior with shells.

116

PART FOUR

A Lake in the Landscape, 1755-1785

Capability Brown's design for the Cascade at Blenheim, 1763.

He who landscapes last . . .

'Water is the most interesting object in a landscape, and the happiest circumstance in a retired recess; captivates the eye at a distance, invites approach, and is delightful when near; it refreshes an open exposure; it animates a shade; chears the dreariness of a waste, and enriches the most crouded view: in form, in style, and in extent, may be made equal to the greatest compositions, or adapted to the least: it may spread in a calm expanse to sooth the tranquillity of a peaceful scene; or hurrying along a devious course, add splendor to a gay, and extravagance to a romantic, situation.'

'Water is either running, or stagnated.'

Thus did the invaluable Thomas Whately sum up the attitude of the 1760s to water, about to become an essential ingredient in every landscaped park in England.

> In the front of Blenheim was a deep broad valley, which abruptly separated the castle from the lawn and the plantations before it; even a direct approach could not be made, without building a monstrous bridge over this vast hollow.
>
> This valley has lately been flooded; it is not filled; the bottom only is covered with water; the sides are still very high, but they are no longer the steeps of a chasm; they are the bold shores of a noble river. The same bridge is standing without alteration; but no extravagance remains; the water gives it propriety. . . . The middle arch is wider than the Rialto, but not too wide for the occasion.

The man who built the monstrous bridge was John Vanbrugh, and the man who made the canal beneath it Henry Wise. The man who flooded the valley, giving the landscape the shape it has today, was Lancelot Brown. He was born in Northumberland in 1715, and was educated at Cambo School. He worked first as under gardener at the great house at Kirkharle; then, moving south, at Wotton, Buckinghamshire. A year later, in 1740, he went to Stowe, where he had charge of the kitchen garden. One of his other duties was to show the nobility and gentry round the garden, and it was in this way that he came in contact with those who were to become his clients. From his habit of saying, when consulted, 'There are great capabilities here', he has become known to us as

In order to form the great expanses of water which featured so often in Capability Brown's landscapes, streams and rivers had to be dammed. Cascades were introduced in various forms. (*Left*) The water leaves the great lake at Bowood over a cascade of artificial rockwork, 1762. (*Right*) The Gothick cascade disgorges the water into the lake at Dodington, designed by Brown in 1764.

Capability Brown. His youngest son, whom he was able to send to Eton, was known to his schoolmates as 'Capey'.

His landscapes were conceived largely in practical terms. His gradients were for sheep and ploughmen, his immense sweeps of trees—on one estate he planted a hundred thousand—were for posterity. He turned architect in 1751 and, though he designed at least one Orangery and a Gothick church, incidental buildings were no part of his art. He organised the English landscape into great natural curves, crowned them with clumps of trees, natural forest and boundary screens. He used mostly elm, oak, beech, lime, Scots fir, plane, larch and the Cedar of Lebanon, the first five of which were native. He became Royal Gardener to George III in 1764.

It was the asymmetrical, flowing style of the early Celtic artists on a huge scale. His landscapes were best seen on horseback. Water was introduced to almost every park he touched, by damming streams or flooding marshes, elaborately natural cascades being made at one end or the other. Rarely, if ever, was he asked to begin on virgin land. Many of his effects were achieved only after the destruction of earlier, more formalised, decorated gardens. Of him, Horace Walpole wrote: 'Such was the effect of his genius that he will be least remembered. So closely did he copy Nature that his works will be mistaken for it.'

Thomas Whately visited Stowe at this time.

The whole space is divided into a number of scenes, each distinguished with taste and fancy; and the changes are so frequent, sudden, and complete, the transitions so artfully conducted, that the same ideas are never continued or repeated to satiety. These gardens were begun when regularity was in fashion; and the original boundary is still preserved, on account of its magnificence; for round the whole circuit, of between three and four miles, is carried a very broad gravel walk, planted with rows of trees, and open either to the park or the country; a deep-sunk fence attends it all the way, and comprehends a space of nearly four hundred acres. But in the interior scenes of the garden, few traces of regularity appear; where it yet remains in the plantations, it is generally disguised; every symptom almost of formality is obliterated from the ground; and an octagon basin in the bottom, is now converted into an irregular piece of water, which receives on one hand two beautiful streams, and falls on the other down a cascade into a lake.

The back of the Dodington Cascade, where the water is channelled in from the river.

Brown's Gothick conservatory at Burghley, 1754.

Brown's Gothick gazebo at Tong, in Shropshire, 1765.

Heveningham Hall, landscaped by Brown in 1781.

Brown's great lake at Blenheim, 1763, which replaced Vanbrugh's formal canal and, in the process, submerged a large section of Vanbrugh's great bridge.

The plants on this account were purchased for the Wilderness at Petworth, in Sussex.

Mr. Lance.^tt Brown of John Williamson

1753 Apl. 11th

40 Scotch firrs 13 foot & upwards	1	10	0
20 Spruce Do	1	—	—
30 Laurels 7/6d 2 Matts 2/– Cart 5/–	—	14	6

1755 March 5th

80 Sweet Briars 19/– 30 Honeysuckles 7/6d	1	6	6
10 Gildirose 2/6d 3 Syringoes 7/6d 20 Spa Broom 5/–	—	15	—
10 Altheas 2/6d 6 Spireas 18d 10 Double Thorn 15/–	—	19	—
8 Persian Jasamin 2/– 6 Venis Shumacks 3/– 20 Lilac 5/–	—	10	—
5 Grounsil Trees 5/– 20 Thorns of Sorts 1:10/–	1	15	—
10 Virginia Shumach 5/– 10 Virginia Rasbery 2/6d	—	7	6
4 Tamarisk 4/– 5 Oriental Collutea 5/– 6 Cochgigrea 3/–	—	12	—
6 Cytisus 18d 35 Larch 8 foot 1:15/– 20 Western plane £1	2	16	6
20 Acacia 8 foot 1:10/– 5 Stand^d Almonds 5/–	1	15	—
5 S^d Dbb peach 10/– 6 Bird Cherry 3/– 3 Catalpha 4/6d	—	17	6
6 Dbb Cherry 3/– 20 privets 5/– 20 Sd. pilters shrub 5/–	—	13	—
10 Black Berryd Alder 2/6d 7 American Maples 14/–	—	16	6
4 Sea Buckthorns 4/– 10 Hypericum 2/6d 10 Mezerion 10/–	—	16	6
4 Trumpet Flowers 6/– 10 Arbutus 1:5/– 80 roses of Sorts 30/–	3	1	—
6 Larger Matts 6/– a flasket 18d Cart 6/–		13	6

April 23d

3 Savin 18d 3 Arbor Vitae 3/–			
6 Chinese Arbor Vitae 30/–	1	14	6
6 Portugal Laurels 12/– 8 Candle Berry Tree 16/–	1	8	—
6 Butchers Broom 18d 6 Germander 4/6d	—	6	—
10 Ilex 5/– Basket 6d Matt 1/– Carr 2/–	—	8	—

1756 March 2d

60 Sweet Bryar 15/– 40 Larch 6 foot £2	2	15	—
5 Rosa Mundi 15d 5 Maidens Blush 2/6d		3	9
6 Dbb White 18d 3 Belgick 18d 6 Damask 18d	—	4	6
5 Virgin 2/6d 6 province 18d 6 Monthly 18d	—	5	6
4 York and Lancaster 2/– 4 Childing 2/–	—	4	—
5 Tamarisk 15d 10 Althea frutex 5/–	—	6	3
20 Laburnum 5/– 50 Lilac of sorts 15/–	1	—	—
20 Acacia £1 2 Matts 2/– Carr^g 3/–	1	5	—

1757 March 30th

100 Planes 6 to 8 foot 50/– Matt & Carr^g 3/–	2	13	—

	£33	13	0

Dec^br the 28th 1757
Mem: that this Acct. was paid
with my own and is to be charged
to the Earl of Egremont

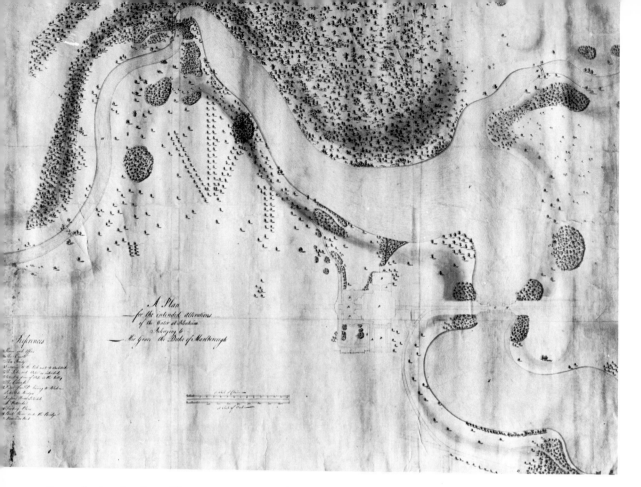

A Plan
for the intended alterations
of the Water at Blenheim
belonging to
His Grace the Duke of Marlborough

References

Brown's plan for the park at Blenheim.

There we can see the hand of Lancelot Brown; the Octagon Basin was Bridgeman's. Brown appears to have left the numerous buildings where they were. Two elegant Doric pavilions, a noble Corinthian arch, an open Ionic rotunda, a pyramid, the Queen's pillar, the King's pillar, are mentioned by Whately. They can all be seen from the rotunda, but 'each belongs peculiarly to some other spot; they are all blended together in this, without meaning; and are rather shewn on a map, than formed into a picture'.

Kent's building, 'three pavilions, joined by arcades, all of the Ionic order', is there; the temple of Bacchus, the temple of Friendship, the temple of Ancient Virtue, and of the British Worthies, all survive. 'The vivacity of the stream, the sprightly verdure of the greenswerd, the variety of the trees, give it [all] a gaiety, which the imagination can hardly conceive, or the heart wish to be exceeded.'

'Certainly when all are seen by a stranger in two or three hours, twenty or thirty capital structures, mixed with others of inferior note, do seem too many. . . . It may be difficult to determine which to take away.'

The problem, now, was to decide which genius to consult, and of which place.

124

An Air of Chearful Serenity

One of the great discoveries of this time was that it was totally unnecessary to build ruins. England was covered with them, the remains of magnificent castles and superb abbeys, systematically plundered over the years for their building materials. There must be more ruins of this kind in England than in any other country in the world.

It was an era of calm, of military success abroad, expanding agriculture and industry at home. The Stuart uprisings of 1715 and 1745 had been quelled. It was a hundred years since the end of the Civil War and two hundred since the Dissolution of the Monasteries. It was possible to look back on these disturbed times with a certain air of patronage and to regard their relics as if they were, indeed, features in a painted landscape.

One of the first landscapes arranged specifically to include real ruins was at Rievaulx in Yorkshire. A wide grass terrace was made—indeed it appears that the top of a hill was levelled—a rotunda was made at one end and a temple, which was in fact a handsome room for dining in, at the other. The word 'picnic', the origin of which is unknown, dates from 1748, and from about this time much of English social life took place

The Terrace above Rievaulx Abbey, in Yorkshire, begun by Thomas Duncombe III in 1750. The plan to link the terrace at Duncombe with this one at Rievaulx by means of a viaduct across a ravine was finally abandoned.

View from the Banqueting House at Rievaulx.

The ruins of Rievaulx Abbey in the valley below.

outside, in the garden or in the park. Portraits of families were painted sitting on lawns in front of the house, walking in the fields, or by the lake.

Walking from the temple to the rotunda at Rievaulx—something one can still do with great pleasure today—the hillside below was covered with trees, through which vistas were cut to give different 'picture' views of the ruins of Rievaulx Abbey, which rose at the foot of the hill. At Stourhead, the mediaeval Cross from Bristol—rescued from the City Fathers who wished to demolish it, if not quite to make a new roundabout or another public convenience, at least because it was considered to be very much in the way—was erected in its present position. Lancelot Brown was commissioned to treat the ruins of Roach Abbey 'with Poet's feeling and with Painter's eye'; and, in 1768, at Studley Royal, the ruins of Fountains Abbey were included in the prospect.

The Reverend William Gilpin, of whom we shall hear more later, visited Studley on his way to the Lakes in 1772. Of the original canal and moon ponds, he said:

On the whole, it is hard to say, whether nature has done more to embellish Studley; or art to deform it. Much indeed is below criticism. But even, where the rules of more genuine taste have been adopted, they are for the most part unhappily misapplied. In the point of opening views, for instance, few of the openings here are simple, and natural. The artifice is apparent. The marks of the sheers, and hatchet, are conspicuous in them all.

On the subject of the newly-included ruin, he wrote:

The very idea of giving finished splendor to a ruin, is absurd. How unnatural, in a place, evidently forlorn and deserted by man, are the *recent* marks of human industry! . . . the *restoration* of parts is not enough; *ornaments* must be added: and such incongruous ornaments, as disgraced the *scene*, are disgracing also the *ruin*. The monk's *garden* is turned into a trim parterre, and planted with flowering shrubs: a view is opened, through the great window, to some ridiculous figure, (I know not what; Ann Bolein, I think, they called it) that is placed in the valley; and in the central part of the abbey-church, a circular pedestal is raised out of the fragments of the old pavement; on which is erected—a mutilated heathen statue!!!

127

The ruins of Fountains Abbey had to wait several decades before they could be incorporated in John Aislabie's Great Garden at Studley Royal. It was not until 1768 that William Aislabie managed to buy the neighbouring estate of Fountains Hall and with it the Abbey. It now forms the culminating part of the whole design.

It is a difficult matter, at the sight of such monstrous absurdities, to keep resentment within bounds. . . . A legal right the proprietor unquestionably has to deform his ruin, as he pleases. But tho he fear no indictment in the king's bench, he must expect a very severe prosecution in the court of taste. . . . A ruin is a sacred thing. Rooted for ages in the soil; assimilated to it; and become, as it were, a part of it; we consider it as a work of nature, rather than of art. Art cannot reach it.

From An Inventory *taken at Holkham, in Norfolk, on August the 31st, 1761:*

In the Pleasure Ground and Orangery
20 Small Winsor Chairs
6 Compass Back Chairs
20 Barrow Chairs
3 Double Seated Chairs

Plants and Trees in Tubbs and Potts

250 Pines in Potts [pineapples]
4 Citrons in Tubbs
46 Orange Trees in Tubbs
9 Lemon Trees in Potts
3 Broad Leafed Myrtles in Tubbs
25 Double and Single Leafed Myrtles in Potts
70 Seedling Oranges in Potts
13 Aloes in Potts

Working Tools and Utensils

11 Scythes
6 Rakes
5 Dutch Hoes
8 English Hoes
8 Forks
3 Jetts
6 Watering Potts
2 Tin Pipes for Watering Pines
1 House Engine
1 Brass Hand Engine
2 Wooden Hand Engines
   [all for water]
3 Leather Pipes
1 Suction Pipe
1 Brass Pipe
1 Rose [for sprinkling]
2 Thermometers
2 Shovells
4 Hammers
1 Hook [Sickle]
1 Hatchet

1 Pair of Garden Sheers
1 Mallett and Pruning Chisell
2 Mattocks
1 Flagg Shovell
1 Edging Tool
2 Pair of Iron Reels with Lines
2 Hand Saws
1 Grindstone and Frame
4 Rubstones
1 Cucumber Cutter
91 Frames Glazed for Mellons
      Pines and Cucumbers
35 Frames for the Fire Walls
21 Hand Glasses
9 Bell Glasses
   Netting in five Parcells
   a Number of old Matts

8 Common Wheel Barrows
2 Water Barrows
3 Water Tubbs
3 Stone Rollers
2 Iron Rollers
5 Boots for Horses to Roll the Garden with
8 Hand Baskets for Frute
1 Large Frute Basket
8 Bushell Baskets
3 Water Pails

If the Reverend William's ideas pointed in one direction, it is important to remember that not everyone was engaged in the quest for simplicity. *A Dissertation on Oriental Gardening*, by Sir William Chambers, published in 1772, was in essence a second version of an essay of 1757. It was then published in *Designs of Chinese Buildings* and one may suppose that a great many opinions there attributed to the Chinese were in fact those of Sir William himself.

> Is it not singular then, that an Art with which a considerable part of our enjoyments is so universally connected, should have no regular professors in our quarter of the world? . . . in this island it is abandoned to kitchen gardeners, well skilled in the culture of sallads, but little acquainted with the principles of Ornamental Gardening. It cannot be expected that men uneducated, and doomed by their condition to waste the vigor of life in hard labour, should ever go far in so refined, so difficult a pursuit.

This was about as close to Lancelot Brown as Sir William chose to approach; but his opinion echoed that of John James, more than fifty years before, when he spoke of

> . . . the very meanest Gardeners, who, laying aside the Rake and Spade, take upon them to give Designs of Gardens, when they understand nothing of the Matter. Unhappy are those that fall into the Hands of such Persons, who put them to a great Expence to plant a sorry Garden; when it costs no more to execute a good Design, than an ill one! The same Trees and Plants are constantly made use of, and produce an ill Effect only through their Bad Disposition.

The situation continues today.
Sir William went on:

> In England, where no appearance of art is tolerated . . . a stranger is often at a loss to know whether he is walking in a meadow, or in a pleasure ground, made and kept at very considerable expence.
>
> At his first entrance, he is treated with the sight of a large green field, scattered over with a few straggling trees, and verged with a confused border of little shrubs and flowers; upon farther inspection, he finds a little serpentine path, twining in regular 'esses' amongst the shrubs of the border. . . .

130

The new village at Milton Abbas, which was designed by Sir William Chambers and modified by Brown about 1775. Whole villages were removed to make way for new gardens and parks in the 18th century.

From time to time he perceives a little seat or temple stuck up against a wall; he rejoices at the discovery, sits down, rests his wearied limbs, and then reels on again, cursing the line of beauty, till spent with fatigue, half roasted by the sun, for there is never any shade, and tired for want of entertainment, he resolves to see no more.

Vain resolution! there is but one path; he must either drag on to the end, or return by the tedious way he came.

The artful style of gardening is, he says, too extravagant a deviation from nature; the simple style too scrupulous an adherence to her. 'One manner is absurd; the other insipid and vulgar.' A judicious mixture of both would be more perfect than either.

But how this union can be effected, is difficult to say. The men of art, and the friends of nature, are equally violent in defence of their favourite system; and, like all other partizans, loth to give up any thing, however unreasonable.

. . . the ax has often, in one day, laid waste the growth of several ages; and thousands of venerable plants, whole woods of them, have been swept away, to make room for a little grass, and a few American weeds.

. . . if the humour for devastation continues to rage much longer, there will not be a forest-tree left standing in the whole kingdom.

Sadly, he did not specify the American weeds. But Sir William, and the Chinese, had a sound common sense indispensable in gardening and it is perhaps unfortunate that he, they, did not achieve a wider influence.

> ... for though the willow ... may grow upon a mountain, or an oak in a bog, yet are not these by any means natural situations for either.

> Gardeners must be men of genius, experience and judgement; quick in perception, rich in expedients, fertile in imagination, and thoroughly versed in all the affections of the human mind.

> They observe, that mistakes committed in this Art, are too important to be tolerated, being much exposed to view, and in a great measure irreparable; as it often requires the space of a century, to redress the blunders of an hour.

September the 12th 1774

Then an Agreement made between the Earl of Scarbrough on the one part & Lancelot Brown on the other, for the underwritten Articles of work to be performed at Sandbeck in the County of York—

To wit

Article the 1st—To compleat the sunk fence which separates the Park from the farm, and to build a wall in it, as also to make a proper drain at the bottom of the sunk fence to keep it dry.

Article the 2nd—To demolish all the old ponds which are in the lawns, and to level & drain all the ground where they are.

Article the 3rd—To drain & level all the ground which is between the above mentioned sunk fence and the old canals mentioned in the Second article. To plant whatever trees may be thought necessary for ornament in that space described in this article & to sow with grass seeds & dutch clover the whole of the ground wherever the turf has been broke up or disturbed by drains, levelling, or by making the sunk fence.

Article the 4th—To make good & keep up a Pond for the use of the stables.

Article the 5th—To finish all the valley of Roach Abbey in all its parts, according to the ideas fixed on with Lord Scarbrough (with Poet's feeling & with Painter's eye) beginning at the head of the Hammer pond, & continuing up the valley towards Loton in the moor, as far as Lord Scarbrough's ground goes & to continue the water & dress the valley up by the present farm house until it comes to the separation fixed for the boundary of the new farm.

N.B. The paths in the wood are included in this description & everything but the buildings.

The said Lancelot Brown does promise for himself & his Heirs, Executors & Administrators to perform or cause to be performed in the best manner in His or their power between the date hereof & December one thousand seven hundred and seventy seven, the above written five articles.

For the Due Performance of the above written five articles the Earl of Scarbrough does promise for himself, His Heirs, Administrators & Executors to pay or cause to be paid at the underwritten times of Payment two thousand seven hundred pounds of Lawfull money of England—and three hundred pounds in consideration of, and for the plans & trouble Brown has had for his Lordship at Sandbeck previous to this agreement.

Lord Scarbrough to find rough timber, four able horses, carts & harness for them, wheelbarrows & planks as also trees & shrubs.

The times of payment:

In June 1775	800
In February 1776	400
In June 1776	400
In February 1777	600
On finishing the works	800
	£3000

Scarbrough
Lancelot Brown

Sir William Chambers was commissioned by the Dowager Princess of Wales in 1757 to lay out Kew Gardens. The three following views are taken from his book— *The Gardens and Buildings at Kew in Surry* published in 1763. In 1757 he had already published his famous essay, *Designs of Chinese Buildings*. *Below*: The Pagoda, with the Alhambra in the foreground and the Mosque in the background.

From The Garden and Buildings at Kew in Surry *by William Chambers, 1763:*

'The gardens at Kew are not very large. Nor is their situation by any means advantageous; as it is low and commands no prospects. Originally the ground was one continual dead flat: the soil was in general barren, and without either wood or water. With so many disadvantages it was not easy to produce any thing even tolerable in gardening: but princely magnificence, guided by a director equally skilled in cultivating the earth, and in the politer arts, overcame all difficulties. What was once a Desart is now an Eden.'

The 'director' referred to was John Stuart, 3rd Earl of Bute.

The following buildings were to be encountered in the course of the circuit walk. The comments are those of Sir William Chambers.

The Orangery 1761
The Temple of the Sun—'This building was begun and finished under my
    inspection in the year 1761.'
The Aviary
The Pheasant Ground 1760
The Chinese Pavilion
Temple of Bellona 1760
Temple of Pan 1758
Temple of Solitude
Temple of Aeolus
House of Confucius—'built a good many years ago, I believe, from the design of
    Mr. Goupy'.
'A semi-octagon seat, designed by Mr. Kent.'
The Theatre of Augusta 1760
Temple of Victory (The Battle of Minden) 1759
The Ruined Arch 1760
The Alhambra
The Great Pagoda 1761—'covered 1762 . . . The design is an imitation of the
    Chinese Taa, described in my account of the Buildings, Gardens &c of the
    Chinese, published in the year 1757.'
The Mosque 1761—'In the way from the Mosque towards the Palace, there is a
Gothic building designed by Mr. Muntz; the front representing a Cathedral.'
The Gallery of Antiques 1757
Temple of Arethusa 1758
The Palladian Bridge—'There is nothing remarkable in the whole, but that it was
    erected in one night.'
The Ruin—'designed and built by me in the year 1759'.
The Temple of Peace

Above: The Orangery, the temples of Aeolus and Bellona, the house of Confucius and the Chinese bridge.

Below: The ruined arch.

Sir William Chambers must be principally remembered for his work at Kew. He assisted the Earl of Bute in making an elaborate Ribbon Walk garden for the Princess of Wales, mother of King George III, along which there were many remarkable buildings. Some of them are still there, though not necessarily where he put them.

If Sir William had reservations about what was going on in the English Garden, Horace Walpole had none.

> In the meantime how rich, how gay, how picturesque the face of the country!
>
> We have discovered the point of perfection. We have given the true model of gardening to the world; let the other countries mimic or corrupt our taste; but let it reign here on its verdant throne, original by its elegant simplicity, and proud of no other art than that of softening nature's harshnesses and copying her graceful touch.
>
> If wood, water, groves, valleys, glades, can inspire poet or painter, this is the country.

The quest for this inspiration was about to begin.

'Nothing is more delusive, than to suppose, that every view, which pleases in nature, will please in painting'

The Reverend William Gilpin, who wrote those words, was a Prebendary of Salisbury and Vicar of Boldre in New-Forest, near Lymington. In 1772 he made a tour of England, fundamentally in search of 'the grand natural scene', which 'will always appear so superior to the embellished artificial one'. In his Preface, he fears that the 'picturesque eye in contemplating the former, will be too apt to look contemptuously at the latter. This is just as arrogant, as to despise a propriety, because it cannot be classed with a cardinal virtue.'

His visit to Studley has already been recorded.

At The Leasowes:

> It was ridiculous to see Naiads [water nymphs] invited, by inscriptions, to bathe their beauteous limbs in *crystal* pools, which stood before the

81 Kitchen Garden by Thomas Robins, about 1740.

82 The Earl of Lincoln and his family by Arthur Devis, about 1751.

83 (*Top*) and 84 (*Bottom*) The Garden at Woodside, about 1755. Paintings by Thomas Robins.

85 South Ormesby Hall. Unknown Artist, about 1770.

86 Blenheim.

87 Petworth.

eye, impregnated with all the filth, which generates from stagnation. . . . Mr. Shenstone's great deficiency lay in not draining, and cleaning his grounds. If he had made his verdure richer, tho at the expence of his buildings, he had shewn a purer taste. But he chose rather to lay out his money on what made most shew, than on what would have been most becoming.

But Mr. Shenstone had done something well.

I cannot leave these scenes without remarking the peculiar beauty of his rocks, and cascades. Of all manufacturers, those of rocks are commonly the most bungling. How often are we carried into the improvements even of people of taste, to see a piece of rock-scenery, consisting perhaps of half a dozen large stones.

To aim at changing the *character* of a country, is absurd.

The plan of Hagley, (if there be any plan) is so confused, that it is impossible to describe it. There is no coherency of parts. One scene is tacked on to another; and any one might be removed without the least injury to the rest.

At Shuckborough, now Shugborough:

It is a pity so generous a design had not been directed by a better taste. . . . There is something rather absurd in adorning a plain field with a triumphal arch . . . above all, the Temple of the Winds, seated in a pool, instead of being placed on a hill, is ill-stationed.

Shugborough in Staffordshire: the Chinese pavilion and bridge and the classical ruin.

Shugborough: general view.

The earliest surviving example of a tree house, at Pitchford Hall in Shropshire—the fake half-timbering was added after 1903.

There was now to be a parting of the ways. What one may call the Garden of Artifice, decorated with Gothick, Classick, Rustick, Chinese, Indian and Egyptian objects, continued to be made well into the next century, increasingly embellished with flowers, flowering shrubs and decorative, as opposed to native, trees. On the other hand, the search for the English Picturesque was to lead to another kind of wild, Romantic garden planted, in general, with native trees and shrubs, and with a suitable quota of fallen logs, ferny dells and horrid chasms.

Pitchford Hall: The gothic interior of 1760.

The Chinese dairy at Woburn.

The source of this kind of landscaping—it cannot really be called gardening, since the object was to create an effect apparently untouched by human hand—was the English Lake District, later to give its name to a Romantic school of poets; and the Reverend William Gilpin may well have been one of the first people to admire it. He did so, however, as a painter, rather than as a landscaper.

> The value of lake-scenery arises rather from the idea of *magnificence*, than of variety.
>
> . . . it cannot be supposed, that every scene, which these countries present, is *correctly picturesque*. In such immense bodies of rough-hewn matter, many irregularities, and even many deformities, must exist, which a practised eye would wish to correct. Mountains are sometimes crouded—their sides are often bare, when contrast requires them to be wooded—promontories form the water-boundary into acute angles—and bays are contracted into narrow points, instead of swelling into ample basons.

It is a natural landscape viewed in terms of the created landscape of Kent and Brown. The practised eye can turn aside an intervening hill:

140

This ill-shaped mountain may be pared, and formed into a better line. . . . To that on the opposite side, a lightness may be given by the addition of a higher summit. . . . On yon bald declivity, which stretches along the lake, may be reared a forest of noble oak.

The sky floating with broken clouds—the mountains half-obscured by driving vapours; and mingling with the sky in awful obscurity—the trees straining in the blast—and the lake stirred from the bottom, and whitening every rocky promontory with it's foam; are all objects highly adapted to the pencil.

Compared with such scenes, how inanimate do the subjects of Canaletti appear! how flat his square canals . . . when opposed to spreading lakes, and sweeping mountains!—the puny labours of men, to the bold irregular hand of nature!

From Observations, on several Parts of England, particularly the Mountains and Lakes of Cumberland and Westmoreland, relative chiefly to picturesque beauty *made in the year 1772, by William Gilpin, A.M.*

On Lakes:
Among the *smaller* lakes of Italy and Switzerland, no doubt there are many delightful scenes: but the *larger* lakes, like those of America, are disproportioned to their accompaniments: the water occupies too large a space, and throws the scenery too much into distance.

The mountains of Sweden, Norway, and other northern regions, are probably rather masses of hideous rudeness, than scenes of grandeur and proportion. Proportion indeed in all scenery is indispensably necessary; and unless the lake, and its correspondent mountains have this just relation to each other, they want the first principle of beauty.

On Rocks:
With regard to the *general form* of rocks, both species, the *smooth*, and the *fractured*, have equal variety. Both have their bold projections—both hang alike over their bases—are rifted into chasms—and shoot sometimes into horizontal, and sometimes into diagonal strata.

The *natural colour* of rocks is either *grey* or *red*. We have of each kind in England; and both are beautiful: but the *grey* rock, (which is the common species in *this* scenery) makes the finest contrast with the foliage either of summer, or of autumn.

I call *red* and *grey* the natural colours of rocks; but more properly they are the *ground* only of a variety of tints. These tints arise from weeds, often make a rich, and very harmonious assemblage of colouring; and the painter, who does not attend to these *minutiae* (we are considering *foregrounds*) loses half the beauty of his original.

On Ruins:

It is not every man who can build a house, that can execute a ruin. To give the stone its mouldering appearance—to make the widening chink run naturally through all the joints—to mutilate the ornaments—to peel the facing from the internal structure—to shew how correspondent parts have once united; though now the chasm runs wide between them—and to scatter heaps of ruin around with negligence and ease; are great efforts of art; much too delicate for the hand of a common workman; and what we very rarely see performed.

Besides, after all, that art can bestow, you must put your ruin at last into the hands of nature to finish. If the mosses and lychens grow unkindly on your walls—if the streaming weather-stains have produced no variety of tints—if the ivy refuses to mantle over your buttress; or to creep among the ornaments of your Gothic window—and if the ash cannot be brought to hang from the cleft; or long, spiry grass to wave over the shattered battlement—you may as well write over the gate, Built in the year 1772.

Nor is the expence, which attends the construction of such a ruin, a trifling difficulty. The picturesque ruin must have no vulgarity of shape; and must convey the idea of grandeur. And no ruins that I know, except those of a real castle, or abbey, are suited to this purpose; and both these must be works of great expence.

Mount Edgcumbe in Cornwall was, along with Stowe, Castle Howard, Stourhead and Blenheim, an essential 'visit' from 1750–1850. It had been transformed, like so many gardens of the time, from a formal layout to make what is still one of the most romantic of English Gardens. The mock ruin, built about 1750. A late 19th-century photograph showing Drake's Island in the middle of Plymouth Sound.

On the Grouping of Animals:
[These were the captions to a number of prints for which there was unfortunately no room.]

This print exhibits a comparison between the lines of the horse and the cow, as objects of picturesque beauty.

This exhibits the same mode of comparison between the bull, and the cow.

These two prints are meant to explain the doctrine of grouping *larger cattle. Two* will hardly combine. There is indeed no way of forming *two* into a group, but by uniting them, as they are represented in the former of these prints. If they stand apart, whatever their attitudes, or situation may be, there will be a deficiency.

But with *three*, you are almost sure of a good group, except indeed they all stand in the same attitude, and at equal distances. They generally however combine most beautifully, when two are *united*, and the third a little *removed*.

Four introduce a new difficulty in grouping. *Separate* they would have a bad effect. Two, and two together would be equally bad. The only way, in which they will group well, is to *unite three*, as represented in the second of these prints, and to *remove the fourth*.

These two prints illustrate the doctrine of grouping *smaller animals*, as sheep, goats, and deer. When they occupy the foreground, as represented in the first, they come under the same rule of grouping, as larger cattle: only a greater number may be introduced. And if the main body be larger, the subordinate group must be so of course.

If they be removed to a *middle distance*, as represented in the other of these prints, the subordinate group is of less consequence; and still of less, the farther it recedes from the eye. The whole is only considered as one body, blended, as it were, and shadowed, or inlightened with the ground: and it is enough, if regular, and disagreeable shapes are avoided.

Mount Edgcumbe:
The Battery on Plymouth Sound below the house.

Such an attitude would have been incomprehensible even to Thomas Whately, who had some interesting remarks to make about the placing of cottages in natural wildernesses; he had found 'the chearful serenity' at Matlock much disturbed 'by the impetuosity of the Derwent'. The Reverend William, however, was quite aware that he was breaking new ground.

> Besides the species of rock just described, there is another, called the *crag*.
> The cascade, which is the next object of our observation, may be divided into the *broken*, and the *regular* fall.

He offers illustrations of different kinds of hill and mountain and says that 'no tree in the forest is adapted to *all* the purposes of landscape, like English oak'.

> Towards Grasmere the whole view is entirely of the horrid kind. Not a tree appeared to add the least chearfulness to it. . . . Of all the rude scenery we had yet visited, none equalled this in *desolation*.

His description of Belle Isle, in Lake Windermere, gracefully demonstrates how the natural could be viewed in terms of the artificial.

> The whole island contains about thirty acres. It's form is oblong; it's shores irregular; retiring into bays, and broken into creeks. . . . Formerly the whole island was one entire grove. At present it is rather bare of wood; though there are some large oaks upon it.
> One of its greatest beauties arises from an irregular little ridge, which extends from one end to the other.
> The lake performs the office of a sunk fence, the grandeur of each part of the mainland being called in, by turns, to aid the insignificance of the island.
> The middle part of the island, with a few clumps properly disposed, might be neat pasturage, with flocks and herds; which would contrast agreeably with the rough scenery around. The house, at present, stands too formally in the middle of the island. It might stand better near the southern promontory.

Westmorland, which Daniel Defoe called 'the most barren and frightful County in England', was about to enjoy a great vogue.

Above Mount Edgcumbe: The 'ruined' arch on the coast walk.

Below Mount Edgcumbe: The Italian Garden designed in the second half of the century.

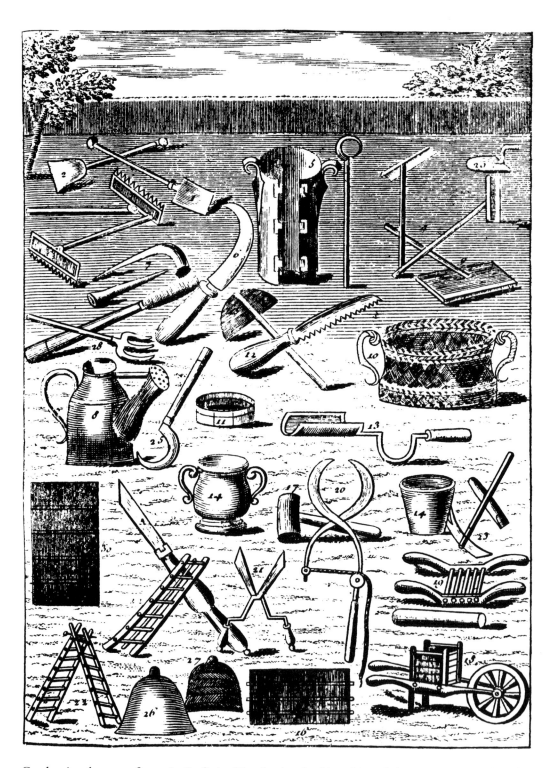

Garden implements from *Le Jardinier Fleuriste* by *Le Sieur Liger d'Auxerre* 1787.

KEY

1 Spade; **2** Shovel; **3** Rakes; **4** Rakers [for keeping the garden clear of weeds]; **5** Displanter [for moving plants to be transplanted]; **6** Pruning knife; **7** Dibbles [for planting seedlings]; **8** Watering pot; **9** Beetle [for smoothing the walks]; **10** Flower Basket; **11** Sieve; **12** Saw; **13** Transplanter [for digging up plants to be transplanted]; **14** Garden Pots; **15** Plainer or Rabot [for smoothing after raking]; **16** Panniers of straw [for protecting seedlings from frost]; **17** Mallet; **18** Wheelbarrow; **19** Handbarrow [for small loads]; **20** Caterpillar shears [the clip the tuft in which the caterpillars lodge]; **21** Garden Shears; **22** Double Ladder [for arbours and high ledges]; **23** Pickaxe; **24** Rolling Stone [a kind of roller]; **25** Hook; **26** Glass Bell [or cloche]; **27** Straw Bell [to protect seedlings from the sun]; **28** Garden Fork; **29** Trowel; **30** Hurdle [riddle or gravel sieve].

PART FIVE

A Picturesque Paradise,
1785–1840

Design from the *Red Book* for Holkham by Humphry Repton 1812.

AN
ACCOUNT
OF A
COTTAGE AND GARDEN
NEAR TADCASTER.

WITH

OBSERVATIONS

UPON LABOURERS HAVING FREEHOLD COTTAGES
AND GARDENS,

AND UPON A PLAN FOR SUPPLYING COTTAGERS
WITH COWS.

PRINTED AT THE DESIRE OF THE SOCIETY
FOR BETTERING THE CONDITION, AND
INCREASING THE COMFORTS OF THE POOR

LONDON:

PRINTED FOR T. BECKET, BOOKSELLER, PALL-MALL
1797.

PRICE ONE SHILLING A DOZEN.

'The great specific of the age for the sorrows of the poor was charity'

Cottage gardens changed very little over the years.

The Comfort of a Gravel Walk

'Let us, then, begin by defining what a garden is, and what it ought to be. It is a piece of ground fenced off from cattle, and appropriated to the use and pleasure of man: it is or ought to be, cultivated and enriched by art, with such products as are not natural to this country, and, consequently, it must be artificial in its treatment, and may, without impropriety, be so in its appearance; yet, there is so much of littleness in art, when compared with nature, that they cannot well be blended; it were, therefore, to be wished, that the exterior of a garden should be made to assimilate with park scenery, or the landscape of nature; the interior may then be laid out with all the variety, contrast, and even whim, that can produce pleasing objects to the eye.'

Humphry Repton, from whose *Theory and Practice of Landscape Gardening* these words are taken, was born in 1752 at Bury St. Edmunds, where his father was Collector of Taxes. He received a grammar school education and later went to Holland, as he was intended by his family to join one of the many firms in Norwich then engaged in trading with the Dutch. He returned at sixteen, an accomplished draughtsman, equipped with many social graces.

He did not join the firm in Norwich. He spent the next five years gardening, studying botany and entomology, and making drawings both of natural scenes and the many country seats in the neighbourhood. He went briefly to Ireland as confidential secretary to the owner of Felbrigg—to whose library he had at all times had access—when he was appointed Chief Secretary to the Lord Lieutenant.

Returning to England, he settled near Romford and lost most of his money in a business speculation. It was at this time, 1788, that he decided that he had all the qualifications to become a landscape designer. The story is that he reached this decision in the middle of one night; he wrote to his friends the next morning, announcing that he was now a landscape gardener, and his success was instant. It continued. The son of Capability Brown, who died in 1783, now Mr. Lancelot Brown, M.P., gave Repton access to his father's papers, tacitly admitting him as his successor; and, to an extent, Repton did consider himself in this role.

149

When Humphry Repton was consulted by a client, he compiled a Red Book, so called because the covers were usually red. It contained a survey of the property in its present state, perhaps a map of the proposed changes, a sketch of the site with the changes shown by cut-outs, if this were possible, or by another sketch showing what he intended. They were accompanied by an account of the changes he wished to make and why he wished to make them.

These are extracts from the Red Book for Garnons, in Herefordshire, dated at Garnons, February 16, 1791, and at Hare Street by Romford, July 1791. Bound in leather, it is, of course, brown.

Situation

The delightful bank on which the house is situated, looking towards the south, and commanding the most interesting and varied scenery, is such as fully justifies a continuance of the house near the present site; and independant from any consideration of convenience in availing ourselves of part of the present buildings, and of the walks which are already made in the vicinity of the house; I am of opinion, that there is no situation more desirable for the new house, than the ground I marked out a few yards forwarder South east of the old house, allowing a sufficient space for convenient yards and offices. The situation tho' high is not more exposed than must be unavoidable on the banks of so extensive a vale, and in speaking of the plantations I shall observe how far this exposure may be remedied and counteracted.

Repton here takes an unadorned 18th-century cottage and transforms it into a 'picturesque' one. From the Repton *Red Book* for Wimpole, in Cambridgeshire.

Character

The Character of a place will take its distinguishing marks from the united consideration of its situation and the extent of territory surrounding.

Both these at Garnons require a degree of Greatness which neither the house nor Grounds at present indicate. It is not necessary to build a palace to produce the Character of Greatness, but a house which is the seat of Hospitality, and where according to the custom of Herefordshire, not only the neighbouring families but even their servants and horses may receive a welcome, must necessarily form such a mass of building as will give an air of Greatness to the general appearance. I am particularly happy in this instance that I act in concert with such acknowledged powers as those of James Wyatt Esq.ʳ whose sentiments I deliver as well as my own in the following page.

The House

A Situation where the house will always be an object at a great distance to all the Country, illumined by the south sun, and where only one front can ever be seen, being embosomed in wood and sheltered by hill above it, should have such an extent of front as may make the buildings not appear less considerable than they are. Custom and Habit makes us expect in Grecian architecture a correspondence in the two sides of a building, but in what is generally called the Gothic stile, the same causes reconcile us to variety, for there is no instance of a Gothic building with strictly corresponding parts; yet there is a harmony preserved in these seemingly discordant parts, which produces with skilful management at a certain distance, the effect of a magnificent *whole*.

151

Approach

It is very essential that the Approach from Hereford should be marked with all the consequence of which the place is capable; . . . the Approach which I propose, and have marked on the map, has every advantage to recommend it. We quit the high road at a sufficient distance; a single Lodge will attract notice and point the way. We here enter the park betwixt two plantations, the depth of which will be impossible for the Eye to distinguish, we burst upon the Lawn at a most interesting point of view, a very extensive park scene presents itself to the west, and as we proceed the house appears in full magnificence, displaying all its length of front, with the accompaniment of the adjacent buildings.

Water

As an object of beauty there can be no room to hesitate about destroying the pond in front of the present house, but as an object of convenience it may deserve consideration . . .

There is another place in which I can with more confidence advise that a small piece of water should be formed, it will be necessary to raise the road to some height as a causeway over the wet part of the meadow, and very little additional expence will form a dam to support a small pool which will easily take the shape I have described on the map; so small a piece of water in itself would be very inconsiderable in the extensive Park of Garnons, but its effect may be very important especially as I am of opinion that some reach of the river Wye may be rendered visible from the house with proper management, or at least a part of the wet moor may be made to shew an apparent continuation of River.

Sheringham, on the north Norfolk coast, from Repton's *Red Book* of 1812. The orangery, which was not built, is nevertheless shown in a position close to the house.

Garden Walks

The first object of improvement ought to be *Convenience*; and *Beauty* should adapt itself to *that*: from this consideration I think a Kitchen Garden cannot be too near a house if it is not seen from it, but as it is impossible at Garnons to have the Garden contiguous to the dwelling, it is necessary that it should be as near as the situation will permit, and that the most pleasing and easy line of communication be made from the house to the Garden: . . . The House stands on a terrace a few feet above the level of the road, and along this terrace a walk leads to the Garden over the gate way by which carriages go from the house to the Stable Court: the idea is in some degree new, its effect will be very picturesque, as well as convenient; and the boldness of the Ground with the romantic scenery, justifies the singularity of the expedient.

Of Deceptions

It may perhaps be objected that such a deception as that which I have hinted is beneath the dignity of a place like Garnons, but it is the business of Taste to deceive, if so hard an appellation deserves to be given to all those efforts, by which Art endeavours to conceal her own works, and make them appear the products of Nature only.

Every attempt to improve may be called a deception, we plant a hill to make it appear higher than it is, we open the banks of a natural river to make it appear wider, we sink a fence betwixt one Lawn and another to give imaginary extent, without the necessary confinement; and every piece of artificial water, whether it take the shape of a Lake, a river, or a pool, must be a deception or it will fail of being agreeable.

One of Repton's proposals in his *Red Book* for Holkham.

Such a pool as I have recommended, small as it is, will give variety to the drive which I suppose to pass along its bank, and from the high road it will appear more important than it really is: if to these advantages can be added, that from the house its glittering appearance will occasionally induce the stranger to suppose he sees a reach of the Wye, which he knows must flow at no great distance, the deception is surely very allowable.

The Park

There being no other word by which to distinguish that portion of Lawn and Wood which surrounds a house, I generally use the word *Park* whether it be inclosed by a pale or not, and whether it support Sheep Deer or Grazing Cattle. A Greatness of Character is necessary to be preserved in the Park as well as in the buildings of Garnons, but this is not to be done by extent alone, altho' an apparently uninterrupted unity of domain contributes very much to the consequence and dignity of a place. The present Turnpike Road is certainly too near to allow a sufficient depth of Lawn to the south. . . . I do not hesitate therefore in advising that the opportunity should not be neglected of directing the Course of the turnpike from the dotted orange line in the map, to that marked below it.

The view of the sea from Repton's *Red Book* for Luscombe, Devon. 1799.

154

The Drive

[This refers to the drive through the grounds suitable for carriages. What we would now call the drive, Repton refers to as The Approach.]

I have already observed the necessity of interrupting the line of plantation or belt which I suppose to surround the Lawn to the south, but it will by no means be so effectually done as by a very bold projection or tongue of planting, which may include within its bosom the whole or part of what I believe is now an orchard, such a plantation will give those deep recesses of Lawn which leave to the imagination to fix their limits, while the eye as it passes over the tops of the trees unites the masses of wood with the distant hedge rows beyond, forming that vast expanse of timber on the plain, which is as necessary to give importance to Garnons, as extent of Lawn or sweep of hanging wood. . . . From this part of the drive which I have marked by a darker green line, the house will have a most delightful Effect, and it will be much oftener used than the more wild and romantic continuation of the drive over the hills at the back of the house, because I suspect there will be found some difficulty in removing all ideas of danger from the pleasure which such a drive would excite.

The view towards the house at Luscombe, designed by John Nash, showing Repton's planting of the park.

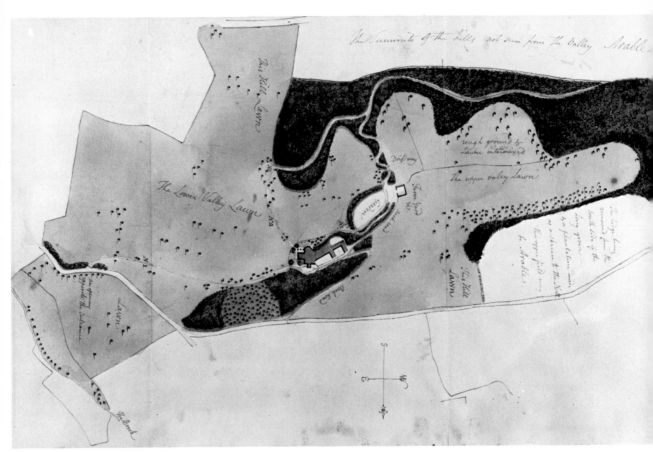

Repton's plan for the park at Luscombe.

He accepted the landscape of Brown, who must be regarded as the inventor of the English park, and worked in his idiom, though his trees were placed quite differently and he worked on a more intimate scale. But his principal contribution must be that he brought back the flower garden to surround the house. Very often, this was made on a terrace, fenced or balustraded, which served the function of a HaHa. The sheep and cows which, apparently, could walk into the hall of a house in a Brown landscape, so closely did the fields approach the house, could not even appear to do so in a Repton one.

His gardens, as opposed to his landscapes, were 'artificial'. The flower beds were often circular; he placed groups of shrubs in lawns as he placed groups of trees in fields; the grass was rolled and neatly cut; the walks were of gravel; there were conservatories and garden houses. His gardens flowed; harmony and unity were what he strove for.

'Congruity of style, uniformity of character, and harmony of parts with the whole, are different modes of expressing *unity*, without which no composition can be perfect.'

156

The Picturesque School—which we may regard as having been founded by the Reverend William Gilpin, but now represented by two Herefordshire squires, Sir Richard Payne Knight and Uvedale Price Esquire (later Sir Uvedale)—found much to criticise in all this. Their particular target was Capability Brown, about whom neither had one good word to say. Their particular theory, reduced rather closer to absurdity than they might perhaps have liked, was that the 'beautiful', which was smooth, could not be 'picturesque', which was rugged—that is to say, that a gardened garden was no subject for a painting, and especially not the contrived landscapes of Brown, with their huge expanses of grass.

> I have frequently heard it wondered at, that a green lawn, which is so charming in nature, should look so ill when painted. It must be owned, that it does look miserably flat and insipid in a picture; but that is not entirely the fault of the painter, for it would be difficult to invent any thing more wretchedly insipid, than one uniform green surface dotted with clumps, and surrounded by a belt.

This was one of the many opinions of Uvedale Price; but in other ways his theories seem to have been close to Repton's.

> . . . the difficulties in gardening, as in other arts, do not lie in forming the separate parts, in making upright terraces and fountains, or serpentine walks, plantations, and rivers, but in producing a variety of compositions and effects by means of those parts, and in combining them, whatever they may be, or however mixed, into one striking, and well connected whole.

Their writings, however, obliged Repton to reply. In a letter of remarkable dignity, dated the 1st of July 1794, to Uvedale Price, which he published, he said:

> . . . *in whatever relates to man, propriety and convenience are not less objects of good taste, than picturesque effect*; and a beautiful garden scene is not more defective because it would not look well on canvas, than a didactic poem because it neither furnishes a subject for the painter or the musician.

> The neatness, simplicity, and elegance of English gardening, have acquired the approbation of the present century, as the happy medium

Thomas Hearne's illustrations to Richard Payne Knight's poem *The Landscape*, showing a typical Brownian landscape, a mild and gentle interpretation of nature and the rough and rugged view of nature proposed by Knight. Knight collected Claude's drawings (now in the British Library) which, because they are drawings from nature, show a marked difference from Claude's idealised landscape paintings which influenced Kent.

betwixt the wildness of nature and the stiffness of art; in the same manner as the English constitution is the happy medium betwixt the liberty of savages and the restraint of despotic government.

No man can hesitate between the natural group of trees, composed of various growths, and that formal patch of firs which too often disfigures a lawn, under the name of a clump; but the most certain method of producing a group of five or six trees, is to plant fifty or sixty within the same fence; and this Mr. Brown frequently advised, with a mixture of firs to protect and shelter the young trees during their infancy; but unfortunately, the neglect or bad taste of his employers would occasionally suffer the first to remain long after they had completed their office as nurses; while others have actually planted *firs only* in such clumps, totally misconceiving Mr. Brown's original intention.

Payne Knight and Price were particularly against 'Clumping and Belting.' Repton defended these practices, though he did admit that a belt could sometimes be too thin.

If a large expanse of lawn happens unfortunately to have no single trees or groups to diversify its surface, it is sometimes necessary to plant them.

. . . if the plantation be judiciously made of various breadth, if its outline be adapted to the natural shape of the ground, and if the drive be conducted irregularly through its course, sometimes totally within the dark shade, sometimes skirting so near its edge as to show the different scenes betwixt the trees, and sometimes quitting the wood entirely to enjoy the unconfined view of distant prospects—it will surely be allowed that such a plantation is the best possible means of connecting and displaying the various pleasing points of view, at a distance from each other, within the limits of the park.

[You] earnestly recommend every gentleman to become his own landscape gardener. With equal propriety might every gentleman become his own architect, or even his own physician . . . and as 'a little knowledge is a dangerous thing', so the professors of every art, as well as that of medecine, will often find the most difficult cases are those, where the patient has begun by *quacking himself.*

159

... both Mr. Knight and you are in the habits of admiring fine pictures, and both live amidst bold and picturesque scenery: this may have rendered you insensible to the beauty of those milder scenes that have charms for common observers. I will not arraign your taste; or call it vitiated, but your palate certainly requires a degree of 'irritation' rarely to be expected in garden scenery; and I trust, the good sense and good taste of this country will never be led to despise the comfort of a gravel walk, the delicious fragrance of a shrubbery, the soul expanding delight of a wide extended prospect, or a view down a steep hill, because they are all subjects incapable of being painted.

'*I think the avowed character of art in the Italian gardens preferable, in garden scenery, to the concealed one now in fashion*': Richard Payne Knight

It is not quite true to say that this controversy raged since, from this distance, Repton, Price and Knight seem to have been basically in agreement; a house should be surrounded by a 'beautiful' garden leading to a 'picturesque' park. *An Analytical Enquiry into the Principles of Taste* by Richard Payne Knight, was in its third edition in 1806; Uvedale Price's *Essays on the Picturesque* were still being published in 1810; and both may have had an effect, directly or indirectly, on the shape the English Garden was to take during the nineteenth century.

Richard Payne Knight put it thus:

When, according to the modern fashion, all around [the house] is levelled and thrown open; and the poor square edifice exposed alone, or with the accompaniment only of its regular wings and portico, amidst spacious lawns interspersed with irregular clumps, or masses of wood, and sheets of water, I do not know a more melancholy object. ... The view from one of these solitary mansions is still more dismal than that towards it; for, at the hall door, a boundless extent of open lawn presents itself in every direction, which the despairing visitant must traverse, before he can get into any change of scenery. ...

For this reason we require, immediately adjoining the dwellings of opulence and luxury, that every thing should assume its character; and

88 Bignonia radicans.

89 Paeonia lusitanica.

90 Tropaeolum.

91 Clematis purpurea.

Flowers from the 1780s.

92 West Wycombe. Painting by T. Daniel, about 1790.

not only be, but appear to be, dressed and cultivated. In such situations, neat gravel walks, mown turf, and flowering plants and shrubs, trained and distributed by art, are perfectly in character; although, if the same buildings were abandoned, and in ruins, we should, on the same principle of consistency and propriety, require neglected paths, rugged lanes, and wild uncultivated thickets. . . . Nevertheless a path with the sides shaggy and neglected, or a picturesque lane between broken and rugged banks, may be kept as clean, and as commodious for the purpose of walking, as the neatest gravel walk. . . .

. . . the hanging terraces of the Italian gardens, which, if the house be placed upon an eminence, with sloping ground before it, may be employed with very good effect; as they not only enrich the foreground, but serve as a basement for the house to stand upon, which at once gives it importance, and supplies it with accompaniments. Such decorations are, indeed, now rather old-fashioned; but another revolution in taste, which is probably at no great distance, will make them new again. . . .

Some few attempts have lately been made to adapt the exterior forms of country-houses to the various character of the surrounding scenery, by spreading them out into irregular masses. . . .

A house may be adorned with towers and battlements, or pinnacles and flying buttresses, but it should still maintain the character of a house of the age and country in which it is erected. . . . Rustic lodges to parks, dressed cottages, pastoral seats, gates, and gateways, made of unhewn branches and stems of trees, have all necessarily a still stronger character of affectation. . . . The real character of every object of this kind must necessarily conform to the use, to which it is really appropriated . . . for to adapt the genuine style of a herdsman's hut, or a ploughman's cottage, to the dwellings of opulence and luxury, is as utterly impossible, as it is to adapt their language, dress, and manners to the refined usages of polished society.

Uvedale Price also pointed the way ahead, by referring to a component of the garden almost entirely ignored for the last sixty years.
'Flowers are the most delicate and beautiful of all inanimate objects; but their queen the rose, grows on a rough thorny bush with jagged leaves,' thus fulfilling, we are left to conclude, the requirements both of the beautiful and the picturesque. It was the flower that was to conquer the nineteenth-century garden.

He was also surprisingly opposed to what he called 'continual flow of outline'.

> Formerly, every thing was in squares or parallelograms; now every thing is in segments of circles, and ellipses: the formality still remains; the character of that formality alone is changed. The old canal, for instance, has lost indeed, its straitness and its angles; but it is become regularly serpentine, and the edges remain as naked and as uniform as before; avenues, vistas, and strait ridings through woods, are exchanged, for clumps, belts, and circular roads and plantations of every kind; straight alleys in gardens, and the platform of the old terrace, for the curves of the gravel walk … the continual and indiscriminate use of such curves, has an appearance of affectation and of studied grace, which always creates disgust.

The Greeks, he mentions here, always used straight lines. It was the early eighteenth-century controversy in reverse. The nineteenth century was to resolve it by using lines of every kind.

A Walk Round Mount Edgcumbe

One of the few gardens approved by Uvedale Price was that of Mount Edgcumbe, opposite Plymouth, which he actually called 'that wonderful place'. It had been there for a long time. When, in 1588, the Duke of Medina Sidonia, in command of the Spanish Armada, sailed past it, he decided that that was where, when the Spanish Conquest of England was completed, he would live.

It was a much-visited garden in the eighteenth century and the seventh edition of what is in effect a guide book was published as late as 1821.

'Many persons of real taste and curiosity, for want of a conductor to direct them in their walk round the grounds, and to explain the different views, arrive at only a small portion of the place, see they know not what, and feel dissatisfied at last with having seen and known so little.'

The grounds were divided into the park, the pleasure-grounds and the gardens.

In the park, the first object of interest was The White Seat. 'From this commanding spot the view is most extensive, and the whole circumjacent country is expanded at your feet.' One could see 'the whole course of the river Tamar as high as Saltash' and 'the irregular summits of Dartmoor' among many other things. 'At this place, the gravel walk ceases, and you enter a grass drive, which is carried round the whole summit of the hill, and conducts straight forward to

Redding Point, whence is discovered a prospect of a totally different description. An unbounded expanse of open sea here bursts upon the sight.'

Further on was the 'wild and finely shaped valley called Hoe Lake'. 'Under a tuft of trees at the bottom stands a Lodge in the cottage style, enclosed in a small garden, with a rustic porch and bench in the front towards the sea.'

The Great Terrace was of grass 'on a perfect level through plantations of fir and other trees, with the sea at a great depth below on your right, till another sharp turn discovers Pickle Combe. This little valley is so regularly scooped out by nature, as almost to bear the appearance of art.'

'At the next corner you find yourself in the midst of a plantation of the finest flowering shrubs . . . covering the whole of the abrupt cliff as far down as the soil allows of vegetation, the sea dashing against the rocks below. . . . The road continues winding amidst this romantic scenery, offering fresh beauties at every turn, till you arrive at The Arch—a building constructed so as to appear like a perforation of the natural rock, which seems here to bar the passage—where a stone seat placed at the edge of an almost perpendicular precipice, commands a fine view over the Sound.

'Notwithstanding the steepness of the cliff, the whole of the Zigzag Walks are so conducted as to be perfectly safe and easy, and numberless benches afford opportunities of rest to the walker disposed to explore and enjoy their infinite variety of beauties.

'From this shade you again unexpectedly burst forth on the rich prospect at a prominent point of the Park, on which stands The Ruin, representing the imperfect remains of a tower with a large gothic window. . . . It is worth while to go up to a platform on the building (which is ascended by an easy stair) from whence a delightful panorama is discovered.

'Instead of re-ascending to the Great Terrace from the Zigzags, . . . take a path cut round the perpendicular cliff under The Arch, (which, though so tremendous in appearance as to be called the Horrors, is yet sufficiently wide to be perfectly safe) and enter the Park below the wood.'

The Cottage, to be encountered next, was 'a small thatched building, fancifully, but tastefully, decorated with a rustic viranda, formed of rugged trees, connected by a balustrade and by festoons of cones, and raised on a rough basement of stone, with rock plants springing up through the interstices; the whole covered with honeysuckles and every sweet flowering creeper'.

In the pleasure grounds the first thing to be noticed was the shrubbery, 'situated on the eminence immediately behind the House, and connected with its southern front'. There was a bower towards the further end of this, but 'in a still more retired part is a semi-circular coved seat, faced and lined with petrifactions and spars from rocks in the neighbourhood, intermixed with shells and various fossils, chiefly the produce of Cornwall. The arbutus and other shrubs grow here with remarkable luxuriance.'

There was also a wide gravel walk, called the Home Terrace, and a valley which, 'from its shape, is distinguished by the name of the Amphitheatre'. The Temple of

Milton, 'an Ionic rotunda, half closed', containing a bust of the poet, stood at the foot of a valley. 'Amongst the fine trees which adorn this valley, several Tulip trees, Oriental and Occidental planes of a remarkable size, a large Cedar of Libanus, and a Carolina Poplar of extraordinary height, ought particularly to be noticed.'

In the garden, the first feature is The Blockhouse, built 'with two or three others, in the reign of Queen Elizabeth, for the defence of the port, and is now a picturesque ruin, partly covered with ivy. . . . No single view, perhaps, exhibits so much variety as this, and from the continual passing of vessels of all descriptions, from the first-rate man of war to the smallest boat, none is so animated and interesting.'

'In this little obscure recess are placed a number of antique cinerary urns and sarcophagi, disposed irregularly about the ground, and on the various points of rock, exhibiting the appearance of a Roman Cemetery.'

The English Flower Garden was 'an irregular piece of ground, of considerable extent, laid out in beds of shrubs and flowers, and traversed by gravel walks, so disposed as to conceal its boundaries, and occasionally to open agreeable vistas, displaying to the best advantage the many beautiful trees that adorn it.'

There was a handsome pavilion in this garden, and it adjoined the French Flower Garden, 'a little square enclosure, bounded by a high cut hedge of evergreen oak and bay, and laid out in a parterre, with a basin and *jet d'eau* in the midst, issuing from rock-work intermixed with shells, and surrounded by *berceaux* [pleached trees] and arches of trellis twined over by all sorts of creeping plants.' There was an octagon room with two conservatories and an urn to the memory of Sophia, Countess of Mount-Edgcumbe, who died in 1806.

Thomson's Seat, a Doric alcove, with lines from 'Autumn' in James Thomson's *The Seasons*, was the last feature before the Italian Garden, or Orangery. 'This plot of ground is encircled by a fine bank of arbutus, laurustinus, and other evergreens, and is disposed in a regular manner with gravel walks, all meeting in the centre, at a bason of water, in the midst of which is a beautiful marble fountain.'

The orange trees were still there, grown in tubs, spending the summer in the garden and the winter in the Orangery. 'On the opposite side of this garden is a terrace, ascended by steps and diagonal slopes . . . and surmounted by a balustrade, on the top of which stands the Apollo of the Belvidere, between Venus of Medici and Bacchus.'

The anonymous author admits that 'he is fully sensible that persons who have never seen the place, could form no accurate idea from this picture'. Much of it remains today, administered by a local authority under the impression that it needs only a great many camellias, and several tons of daffodil bulbs, to render it quite perfect.

It will be observed that the adornments in the park were either Rustick or Gothick, while those in the garden and pleasure grounds were principally Classick. As a result of the increased contact with China and India, these were about to be joined by the Exotick.

Hawkestone: An escarpment 500 feet above a valley brought into the landscape, about 1806, to accord with the rough and rugged view of Nature held by Knight.

Few gardens were made in England in the true picturesque style, though mention should be made of a magnificent cliff walk, with steep paths, a natural grotto, a natural bridge, a Gothic tower and a classical pillar, now much over-canopied by *Rhododendron ponticum*, at Hawkestone in Shropshire; and the Quarry Garden at Belsay Castle in Northumberland, where the stone used for building the house was removed in such a way that a 'natural' walk was left between cliffs of rock.

Hawkestone: Inside the hillside 'grotto'.

Above: View from the 'grotto' at Hawkestone.

Below: A general view from a contemporary engraving of Hawkestone.

Humphry Repton died in 1818. One of his most complete gardens was made at Ashridge, in Hertfordshire, a Gothick mansion of indisputably picturesque outline. There was a terrace and an 'Embroidered Parterre'; there was a lawn dotted with shrubs which led to the deer park. There was a conservatory and a cloister walk; there was a broad sanctuary with a holy well, apparently a paved area decorated with vases and with a Gothick conduit in the middle.

From here, a winding path led between shrubs to the 'Pomarium and Winter Walk' and to the 'Monk's Garden Restored'. There was an 'Arboretum of Exotic Trees', a magnolia garden and an American garden (probably devoted to azaleas and rhododendrons); there was a grotto and a 'Garden for Rockplants', followed by a mount garden, which seems to have been suggested by the wilderness garden of Francis Bacon. There was a *Cabinet de Verdure*, which we may guess was an enclosure of clipped evergreens, and a rosarium and a fountain.

It was this kind of garden, mercilessly compressed by the next generation, which became the small Victorian garden and which led, in its turn, to the suburban garden of the present day.

A Pocketful of Posies

The Horticultural Society—it did not become Royal until 1861—was founded in 1804. The following year, a paper was read lamenting the fact that 'horticulture . . . appears to have been neglected, and left to the common gardener, who generally pursues the dull routine of his predecessor; and if he deviates from it, rarely possesses a sufficient share of science and information to enable him to deviate with success'. The paper was read by the younger brother of Richard Payne Knight.

Seeds, cuttings and rooted plants from all over the world were now arriving in England, and it became a matter of some urgency not to lose them. The design and construction of greenhouses in which to raise the plants received careful consideration; and later in the century almost every house of any size had a conservatory, not only used for proposals of marriage.

The dahlia, from Mexico where it was a food, arrived in 1789. Originally there were three, a double purple, a rose pink and a scarlet single (*coccinea*) which was sometimes orange or yellow. They hybridised freely and by 1835 there were two hundred garden varieties. It was the fashionable flower of the 1820s. The cactus dahlia, also from Mexico, was not introduced until 1864 and it is, basically, from these four plants that our modern dahlias descend, some of which are rather more beautiful, or picturesque, than others.

Four very important roses from China also appeared about this time. Slater's Crimson China, then called *Rosa chinensis semperflorens*, Parson's Pink China (*Rosa indica vulgaris*), Hume's Blush Tea-scented China (*Rosa indica fragrans*) and Park's Yellow Tea-scented China (*Rosa indica sulphurea*) arrived between 1792 and 1824. The ship carrying the third of these to the Empress Josephine at Malmaison was given a safe conduct from the British Navy then (1809) at war with the French.

These roses did not flower perpetually—that is to say absolutely without stopping as do their descendants, the Floribundas—but they flowered twice and were the ancestors of many wonderful nineteenth-century roses, rich, full and strongly scented, most of which were bred in France.

The fuchsia, from South America, was first introduced into horticulture in the 1820s and became a favourite, almost a compulsory, conservatory plant. The aspidistra came from China in 1824, as did the camellia, the chrysanthemum and the tree-peony. The pelargonium, hybridised from plants from Africa, Australia and Asia Minor, also became a favourite flower at this time. The gardenia, from America, was grown in hothouses, and clarkia, gaillardia, lupins, eschscholtzia, mimulus and pentstemons, also came from America, to be grown as annuals, a word almost unused since the days of Celia Fiennes.

An Encyclopaedia of Gardening (1834) mentions also the hydrangea, from China, the annual balsam, from the East Indies and Japan, mignonette, from Africa, the China Aster—in a particularly good form imported from Germany—the Common Cardinal Flower from Virginia, and the Fulgent and the Splendid Cardinal Flower from Mexico, the greenhouse salvias, nearly all from South America, and alstroemeria, from Peru. In the industrial towns, now beginning to grow, tulips, auriculas, carnations, pinks, anemones, ranunculus, hyacinths and polyanthus continued to be grown, many little local societies being formed to encourage their propagation.

Views of the Quarry Garden at Belsay, in Northumberland. The quarry provided all the stone for the house, stables and houses in the village, and was made about 1806. It is one of the few gardens today that shows Knight's influence.

In 1832, the first hybrid rhododendron appeared. *Rhododendron ponticum*, a native of Ireland before the Ice Age, was re-introduced about 1760 and the American varieties followed very shortly. The Himalayan varieties did not arrive until early in the nineteenth century and the first hybrid was between one of them, *R. arboreum*, and *R. caucasicum*, from Asia Minor. The Himalayan species were not entirely hardy, and an American species, *R. catawbiense*—which can stand 60 degrees of frost—was brought in to produce the Hardy Hybrid Rhododendrons that we know today, and which were such a feature of the Victorian garden.

It was also a time for great improvements in the fruit and vegetable gardens. Hybrid rhubarb—descended from the *Rheum rhaponticum* which John Evelyn saw in the Oxford Physic Garden—was now regularly grown. The Bramley Seedling and the Cox's Orange Pippin both date from this time, as does the progenitor of the modern strawberry. A strawberry from Virginia, which was red but had little flavour, was crossed, in the middle of the eighteenth century, with a Chilean strawberry, which was delicious but was white. After many years of careful selection and patience, Keen's Seedling appeared in 1826, at Isleworth, red and full of flavour, the ancestor of the strawberries we know today.

New varieties of potato and peas were produced, and cabbages which could survive the winter. There were new varieties of pear, cherry, nectarine and damson, many of which are still grown today.

A little of what you fancy does you good

John Claudius Loudon was born at Cambuslang in Scotland in 1783. He was apprenticed to an Edinburgh firm of nurserymen. In 1803 he came to England and was so appalled by the inefficiency of English farming that he set up a school of practical farming, at Great Tew in Oxfordshire. He retired in 1812, a rich man; he travelled widely, and devoted the rest of his life to writing gardening books, editing *The Gardener's Magazine* and the production of *An Encyclopaedia of Gardening*, which first appeared in 1822. After his death in 1843, his wife continued his work until she died in 1858. It was largely through her writing and encouragement that gardening became the essential pastime for women that it has remained ever since.

Loudon must be considered the Father of the English Garden, as this expression is understood today. He was a sincere admirer of Repton and tried to follow his principles, but the total difference in scale—since Loudon addressed himself to The Suburban and Villa Gardener—resulted in an extraordinary confusion both of styles and plants that is known as The Gardenesque, an ugly name for what was frequently an ugly style. Its principal function was to display the skill of the gardener, particularly where the gardener was also the owner.

In *An Encyclopaedia of Gardening*, he wrote:

Objects not beautiful in themselves may become so when combined, from the mere circumstance of their combination forming a whole, and thus producing an effect which is satisfactory to the mind.

Design is quite as essential in landscape-gardening in the natural style as in the ancient style, though it is not openly avowed. Modern landscape-gardening is, to a certain extent, an art of imitation; and as such, it does not aim at producing facsimiles of natural scenery, but scenery composed of natural objects combined according to the rules of art.

There is an essential difference, however, between the landscape-gardener and the painter, which ought never to be lost sight of by the former, and this is, that the materials with which he works are always changing, while those of the artist are fixed.

The hand of man should be visible in gardens laid out in the natural style as in the most formal geometric gardens, because both are equally intended to show that they are works of art, and to display the taste and wealth of the owner.

Here was the licence for the Display Garden of the mid-century, the taste of whose owners quite frequently bore no relation whatever to their wealth. Loudon quotes, among others, Pope, Shenstone, Whately, Price and Knight, but he does not mention Knight's comment on 'the difference between the works of artists of genius, who consult their feelings, and those of plodding mechanics, who look only to their rules'.

Nothing gives more general satisfaction than a neat and comfortable picturesque cottage, fig. 259, with a good garden, in neat order and cultivation; and such buildings may always be applied to some useful

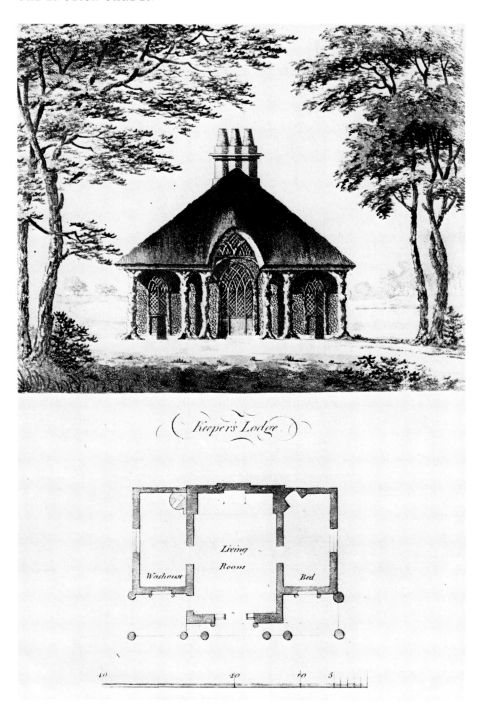

From Plaw's *Ferme Ornée* of 1795 : a design for a keeper's lodge in a park, thatched and with tree trunks for columns and Gothick glassing.

The elaborate aviary at Dropmore, in Buckinghamshire, in the Chinese taste. The trellised pavilion to the right is part of a large trellised walk. About 1820.

purpose, even in the grounds of small villas, or *fermes ornées*. In more extensive scenes, cottages of different styles may be introduced, from that of the Greenlander or Norwegian to the Hindoo; and there can be no reason why a proprietor, if he chooses to go to the expense, and will attend to the comfort of the interior, should not ornament the dwelling of an upper servant in any style he pleases, even that of a Chinese mandarin.

There is no record of a 'Hindoo cottage', but fig. 259 shows an L-shaped stone cottage, with a mullioned oriel window castellated above, a stepped gable terminating in a finial, one tall chimney, a false finialled gable over the attic window and what appears to be an entrance passage consisting of six Perpendicular arches.

Fig. 264, on the other hand, shows a garden in the modern style, about 1834. It is totally flat, divided from gentle hills by groups of trees and an irregular hedgerow. In the distance there is a small church and, on the horizon, a windmill. From the first field a cow and a donkey gaze into the garden; there is a dovecot and what could be a Monkey Puzzle tree. A building emerges from the trees, another church perhaps, or a picturesque

173

Early 19th-century greenhouse at Chislehampton, in Oxfordshire.

cottage. The walks in the garden are straight, and at right angles to one another, and there is a rustic wooden bridge over a straight canal, which has another Monkey Puzzle on its shores. In the garden, there is a circular fountain in a circular basin; a circular seat round a tree; a large stone basket, filled with flowers, in a circular bed whose edges are raised; four urns on pedestals with exotic plants, two with flower beds adjoining. There is a palm tree in a circular bed, three baskets of flowers casually disposed, a sundial, two garden seats, six women and a parrot.

Loudon's avowed purpose was 'to disseminate new and important information on all topics connected with horticulture, and to raise the intellect and the character of those engaged in this art', to do for gardening what Florence Nightingale was to do for nursing some twenty years later. In 1836 he refers to 'the decision of the Horticultural Society of London to admit no young men into the garden as journeymen who had not some school education, and to recommend no one from their gardens for situations as head gardeners who had not been regularly examined in scientific knowledge and received a certificate stating their degree of proficiency.'

Imperceptibly, the gardener took over the garden from the landscape designer and, very frequently, from the owner; the situation which

174

John Nash's Conservatory at Barnsley Park in Gloucestershire, 1806. In 1803, Nash also designed a 'model' village at Blaize Hamlet near Bristol.

obtained between Lord Emsworth and Mr. MacAllister in the novels of P. G. Wodehouse, as late as the nineteen-twenties, was by no means an exaggeration. Imperceptibly, too, a certain solemnity attaches, from this time, to the making of English gardens, which were increasingly not English gardens at all but merely gardens made in England.

If Loudon did not quite understand Landscape Gardening as an art, he fully understood its social implications and its importance as a science. Houses were divided into Seats, of the landed gentry and aristocracy, and Residences. The first-rate suburban property had a park and farmery, and was of not less than fifty acres. A second-rate villa was detached on every side, but was still part of a row. A third-rate one was semi-detached and a fourth-rate one was what we would now call a 'terrace house'.

The section on 'Gardening as a Science' in *An Encyclopaedia of Gardening* is really the largest and it is filled with excellent, practical information. His list of vegetables is enormous, since he includes 'Skirret, Orache, Herb Patience, Rocambole, Rampion, and Alexanders', none of which is grown today. Nasturtiums and marigolds are listed with the 'Pot Herbs and Garnishings', and 'Rhubarb, Pompion and Gourd, Angelica, Anise, Coriander, Caraway, Rue, Hyssop, Chamomile, Elecampane,

175

A suburban villa at Edgbaston in Birmingham. The shrubbery in front of the house is typical.

Liquorise, Wormwood, and Balm' as 'Plants used in Tarts, Confectionery, and Domestic Medecine'.

His list of border plants is also very long. They are listed under their heights and the colour of their flowers, as are shrubs and trees later on; and, as a separate list, the month of flowering.

There was a section on 'Flowers which reach from five to seven feet in height for covering naked Walls, or other upright Deformities, and for shutting out distant Objects which it is desirable to exclude'; 'Plants for concealing Defects on horizontal Surfaces; as naked sub-barren Spots, unsightly Banks &c; Flowers which will grow under the Shade and Drip of Trees; Flowers for Ornamenting Rocks, or Aggregations of Stone, Flints, &c; Evergreen-leaved Plants, Edgings to Beds or Borders, Highly Odoriferous Plants.'

With the invention of the lawn mower in 1830, patented in 1832—a machine which might afford country gentlemen 'an amusing, healthy and useful exercise'—the way was clear for gardening to emerge as the passionate amateur activity it remains to this day.

93 and 94 Garnons before and after. Drawings by Humphry Repton, 1791.

95 and 96 Repton's Designs for Brighton Pavilion, 1806.

J. C. Loudon, founder of *The Gardeners Magazine* in 1822 and author of *Arboretum et Fruticetum Brittannicum* published in 1838. *The Suburban Gardener and Villa Companion*, a book directed mainly at the newly emerging middle class, was to have a profound influence on the English garden for nearly a century. One of the gardens he particularly praised was that of Mrs Lawrence, at Drayton Green, in Middlesex. The plate shows a distinctly Reptonian influence. Loudon republished Repton's *Collected Works* in 1840.

In 1832, Edward Budding, an engineer in a textile factory, patented the first lawnmower. More than any other invention this helped to establish the suburban garden that was beginning to make its appearance as a result of the industrial revolution. In the great gardens of the 19th century, with their vast areas of mown lawns, the rotating blades of Budding's mower were pulled by a horse—the horse wearing overshoes of leather to protect the lawns.

In certain circles, it became almost essential to have designed your own garden in the Gardenesque Style. In that of Mrs. Lawrence, at Drayton Green, in Middlesex, there was a French Parterre, a rustic arch of stone with a cupid on top—near where they often pitched a tent—a rustic arch of wood, with an urn beneath it, through which one could observe the paddock, a pollard vista which could be seen from the lawn and an Italian walk. There were also 3,266 species of plant, among them 500 roses, 200 pansies, 140 pelargoniums, 227 orchids and 140 alpines. By 1838, Mrs. Lawrence had received fifty-three awards from the Horticultural Society.

One must regret that Loudon did not quote the remark of Uvedale Price: 'If it be a high commendation to a writer or a painter, that he knows when to leave off, it is not less so to an improver.'

Perhaps, in his heart, he realised this. Of Mrs. Lawrence's garden he wrote: 'The brilliancy of the flowers, the immense numbers of statues and vases, and the sparkling waters of the various cascades, produced an effect that was perfectly dazzling.'

Loudon did not mean this as a compliment. The next generation was to regard it as essential both to dazzle and to supply the constant 'irritation', as Repton had earlier used the word. There was to be little repose for the eye in the great Victorian gardens.

The Pagoda at Alton Towers, designed by Robert Abraham in 1824.

Repton's Rosarium at Ashridge Park, Herts about 1816.

Mr Fish's 'Truly Elegant Marine *Villa Ornée*' at Sidmouth about 1825.

PART SIX

Perfectly Dazzling,
1840-1914

Osborne House, Isle of Wight, about 1860.

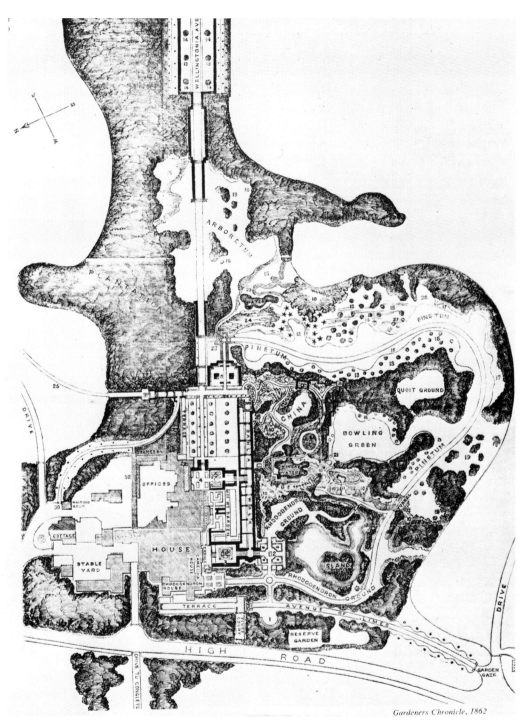

Gardeners Chronicle, 1862

James Bateman began his garden in 1842 in a seemingly unpropitious part of Staffordshire. Dahlia Walks, Camellia Houses and Rhododendron Grounds prove that the collector of plants has arrived on the scene and the exclusion of the countryside, and the public, emphasises a desire for privacy in an increasingly populated country.

'A Grand Style of Promenade Gardening'—Shirley Hibberd, The Town Garden, 1859

The garden at Biddulph Grange was begun in 1842, on a bleak Staffordshire moorland which was both rocky and swampy. There was no longer any question of consulting the genius of the place. The purpose now was to create a garden with a character of its own, in harmony with itself, without reference to its surroundings and indeed, in this case, excluding them almost entirely.

As many of the newly imported plants, particularly from North America and the Himalayas, would only grow on sour, or acid, soil, many places in England which the eighteenth century would have regarded as impossible for gardening purposes became intensely desirable, and Biddulph Grange was one of these.

It was a Garden of Artifice, not strictly speaking on the Circuit Walk plan, but not dissimilar. The 'incidents' in this garden were not, however, a series of buildings, but a Chinese Garden, an Egyptian court, a Cheshire cottage, an arboretum, or collection of trees, a pinetum, or collection of pines, both English and foreign. There was a ferny dell with a stream flowing through it, and an avenue originally of Wellingtonias, from North America, but finally of the Himalayan Cedar. It led up the side of

Biddulph: View from the house.

The Chinese Garden
at Biddulph.

The Egyptian entrance
to a Cheshire cottage
through which one
reaches the Chinese
Garden.

the moor, with banks planted above eye level on either side, to give a feeling of enclosure.

There was a formal terrace beside the house and a rhododendron garden, the whole contained within twenty acres laid out in such a way that an impression was given of a far greater extent. The trees and hedges

---

From An Encyclopaedia of Gardening, *edition of 1850, Part III, book iii:*

A mixture of stable-dung, sea-weed, lime, and vegetable mould, which has lain in a heap for three or four months, and has been two or three times turned during that period, will make an excellent manure for most kinds of garden land. Also, cow-dung, hog-dung, and sheep-dung, mixed with soot or with wood-ashes. Pigeon-dung and vegetable mould, well mixed, will also make an excellent manure for heavy land, or even for lighter soils, provided the pigeon-dung be used sparingly.

Neats'-dung and hog-dung, slightly fermented, are very fit and rich manures for light dry soils. For those of a dry absorbent nature none answer better or last longer; because they retain moisture for a greater length of time, and also ferment more slowly than other dungs.

Pigeon-dung, lime, soot, ashes, &c. should never be applied as simples; the quantity required being comparatively small, and the regular distribution of them difficult, without the admixture of other matter. They should be generally applied to a compost of good earth, turf, or sward, or of cow or other dung of a cool nature; applying them in quantity according to the cold or the hot nature of the soil to be manured, allowing the compost a sufficient time to incorporate, and mixing it thoroughly.

Stable-dung, if used as a simple, should not be applied in too rank a state, nor should it be much fermented. It should generally lie in a heap for four or five weeks; during which time it should be turned over once or twice. A ton of it in this state is worth three of that which has been used in a hotbed, and is a year old. This manure, and indeed dung of any kind, when applied as a simple, should never be carried from the heap to the ground till it is to be dug in; as, by exposure to the air, part of its virtues evaporate, and it is the less effectual.

Sea-weed should be applied after landing. If used as a simple, it should be applied sooner than stable-dung, as it very soon corrupts, and its juices being carried down into the soil are lost. If this manure be used as a compound, the heap in which it is placed should be more frequently turned on its account, that none of the juices may be lost, but that the other part of the compost may absorb them.

Horse-dung, and the dung of sheep, deer, and of rabbits, are most eligible for cold wet soils; and all these, or any of these in compost with lime, will be found beneficial. For such soils also, a compost of coal-ashes, pigeon-dung, and lime; or of wood-ashes, whin-ashes, fern-ashes, and stable-dung; or of deer-dung, rabbit-dung, soot, and burnt sward, will make a good manure.

Edward Hussey's garden at Scotney Castle in Kent. His new house, designed by Anthony Salvin in 1842, was built to take advantage of the view of the old castle below. A quarry garden was also formed, but it cannot compare with the quarry at Belsay.

were planted for shelter, to enable an enormous collection of foreign plants to grow there in comfort. In fact, orchids were the great passion of the owner, James Bateman, and he published a magnificently illustrated volume called *Orchids of Mexico and Guatemala*, each one of which had flowered in a hothouse somewhere in England.

It was not a typical garden of its time, except perhaps in its use of evergreens, which were gradually to take over the suburban garden in the course of the century. As early as 1838, Loudon had written: 'Everything in modern landscape gardening depends on the use of foreign trees and shrubs. No residence in the modern style can have a claim to be considered as laid out in good taste, in which all the trees and shrubs employed are not

Victorian planting and sculpture at Grimston in Yorkshire.

either foreign ones, or improved varieties of indigenous ones.' Just as Richard Payne Knight had foretold, the Italian style appeared at this time to do justice to, in particular, the large number of foreign flowers now becoming more and more readily available.

It is a little difficult to see why the Italians should be blamed for this particular style. The Italian Renaissance Garden certainly made use of geometrical shapes, very often outlined in box, and surrounded by gravel. But those gardens were small and the shapes related to one another, which those in the English Italian Garden frequently were not. A certain T. James, writing to the *Gardener's Magazine* in 1839, said: 'We are proud of our natural, or English style, but scores of unmeaning flower beds in the shape of kidneys and tadpoles and sausages and leeches and commas now disfigure the lawn.' The High Victorian Display Garden was to be a development of that.

It was a difficult style within which to work, but at Osborne House, on the Isle of Wight, the Prince Consort laid out, with great success, a garden that is virtually unchanged today. A large, irregular terrace was made with lawns, balustrades, fountains, decorative urns, clipped trees and formal flower beds in an elegant and charming proportion. Steps led down to a smaller terrace enclosed by the L-shape of the upper terrace, which gave on to a huge grass sweep sloping down to the sea. Foreign trees were planted near the house, native ones further away, and the whole arrangement has an atmosphere which makes it easy to understand why Queen Victoria loved it so much.

187

Sir Charles Barry's garden, at Shrubland Hall in Suffolk, for Sir William Middleton.
Above: View up towards the House.

Below: View to the garden.

Nesfield's Terrace at Harewood House with Brown's magnificent park beyond.

In Yorkshire, at Harewood, and in Suffolk, at Shrubland Hall, Charles Barry, architect of the Houses of Parliament, engaged to alter eighteenth-century houses to the current mode, worked with William Andrews Nesfield to create other spectacular terraces. At Trentham, however, the result was less happy and one cannot be quite certain that the Royal Horticultural Society's Gardens at Kensington (1861) were entirely a pleasure to look at.

Parterres by Nesfield still exist, created originally in the Jacobean style of Gervase Markham, using only box edging, but with coloured earths and stones and flowers. At Holkham in Norfolk, at Broughton in Yorkshire, and at Castle Howard, the outlines can still be seen; but at Witley Court in Worcestershire only the great fountains, which he did not design, remain of a very elaborate parterre garden.

Nesfield, who was trained as an Army engineer, worked also at Kew—given by the Queen to the Royal Botanic Society in 1840—with Decimus Burton, architect both of the Palm House and the Temperate House. It was he who restored some of the remaining temples of Sir William Chambers.

189

The huge importation of plants at this time from tropical and semi-tropical lands required special housing in the English climate, nowhere more so than in the Botanic Gardens at Kew, transferred from the Crown to Parliament in 1840. When William Jackson Hooker was appointed Director, in 1844, he employed Decimus Burton to design the Palm House.

Witley Court, Worcestershire, Nesfield's ultimate elaboration of formal 'Italian' gardening.

At Kew, Nesfield laid out the Pagoda Vista, the Broad Walk, and the Syon Vista leading from the Palm House. Of the pond in front of the present Palm House, he wrote: 'The Pond [which] cannot be rendered altogether geometric without considerably lessening it must nevertheless agree in character with the Terraces where it is to be enlarged.' The resulting shape, geometric at one end, 'natural' at the other, can perhaps only be described as unnatural.

'The uneven ground at present in front of the Orangery so distorts the perspective as to render every attempt at harmony with the adopted character abortive unless it is entirely removed . . . alleys and plots are intended for a formal arrangement of the exotic tubs in the summer according to size.'

It was in some ways the theory of the late seventeenth century applied

The Emperor's Walk at Grimston in Yorkshire, designed by William Andrews Nesfield.

Above: The exterior of the Conservatory at Broughton Hall, Yorkshire, with Nesfield's formal garden beyond.

Below: The conservatory, attached to the house and approached by the hall opposite the front door.

97 and 98 Sezincote. Paintings by Thomas Daniell, about 1805.

99 The Pine strawberry.

100 The Downton strawberry.

101 The garden pea.

102 The broad bean.

Vegetables of the 1820s.

A kind of turnip.

104 Different radishes and a carrot.

A turnip.

106 A beetroot with a variegated leaf.

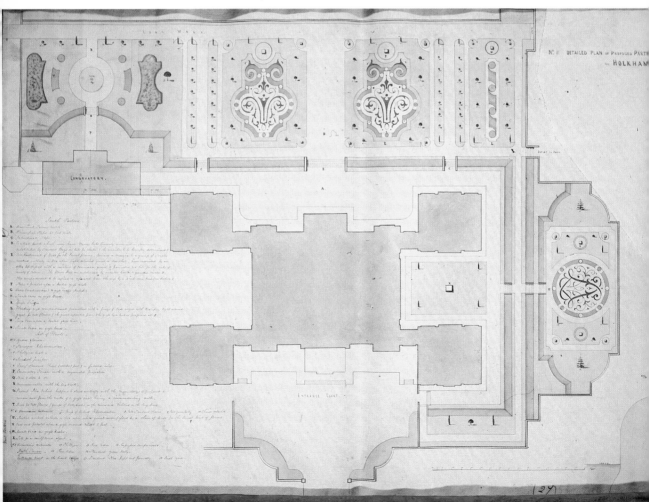

107 (*Top*) Battlesden Park. Painting by G. Shepherd, 1818. 108 (*Bottom*) Nesfield's Plan for Holkham, about 1850.

to the Gardenesque, and this did, perhaps, rescue it from total chaos.

Another remarkable gardener of this time was Joseph Paxton, who started as a gardener's boy in the Horticultural Society's arboretum at Chiswick and rose to be a Member of Parliament, a director of railways and a Knight. As a gardener, he worked principally at Chatsworth, where he was responsible for building The Great Stove—where the first banana to ripen in England was grown—for various rockworks, an arboretum, the aqueduct, the Emperor Fountain and, especially, the Conservative Wall, an elegant arrangement of succession houses. He edited various gardening magazines at different times.

He also designed the glass hall for the Great Exhibition of 1851 in Hyde Park, which was later moved to Sydenham to be known as the Crystal Palace. It was Paxton who designed the elaborate 'Italian' garden round it. That garden has vanished and his influence on gardening has not lasted; but his influence on the design of conservatories must have been considerable.

The Great Stove at Chatsworth, precursor of the Crystal Palace, designed by Paxton in 1836.

Paxton's succession houses at Chatsworth.

It is interesting to note that nearly all the prizes at that Exhibition were awarded for craftsmanship. It is perhaps this that gave rise to the great British myth, still sadly current, that if a thing is beautifully made it is therefore also beautifully designed. However tenuously this idea may be applied to porcelain, motor cars and carpets, it cannot be applied to gardens, many of which look actually worse for being maintained within an inch of their lives.

Irish Yews and the Tamarisk-leaved Savin

The first gnome is thought to have been brought from Germany in the early 1840s. It is still carefully preserved by its fortunate owner. It is made of wood and was one of many disposed around a large rock garden, each one armed with small spade or tiny pickaxe. The rock garden was by this time an essential ingredient both of gentlemen's and ungentlemen's gardens. The first rock garden is thought to have been made at the Chelsea Physic Garden in 1784 by Sir Joseph Banks. He used flints, some lava he had brought back from Iceland and forty tons of old stone from the Tower of London.

By the 1850s, it was time to consider the ungentleman's garden and to write books about it. The industrial middle class, suddenly much larger than before, moved into second- and third-rate villas, in the Loudonian sense, in what we now call the inner suburbs. One of the first people to write about their gardens was Shirley Hibberd, who wrote *The Town Garden, A Manual for the Management of City and Suburban Gardens*. The second edition of this was published in 1859. He was also the author of *Rustic Adornments for Homes of Taste, Garden Favourites, Brambles and Bay Leaves* and several other similar works. His advice in *The Town Garden* is so sensible that one must regret that his work seems not to have been more widely known.

The forecourt, he says, should be simple, elegant, and formal.

Rustic work and rock work are, I consider, in the very worst taste, anywhere in front of a neat villa . . . you will see in front of fine establishments, where there is space for a grand style of promenade gardening, pyramids of brick planted with ferns and trailing plants, piles of stone and wild masses of shrub, even rustic arbours with thatched roofs, and sometimes a few garden seats. . . . I could almost wish that ferns and rockeries had never become fashionable, when I see people pitch them down before the hall door, as if to intimate that they have built their house on the face of a cliff, to which they must look *down*, instead of *up*, and where the vegetation, which would prove delightful a few yards off, is an eyesore and an abortion.

Then we have winding paths, to make butcher-boys giddy, and perplex the stranger . . . and which compel the visitor to make half a tour of the grounds, when his chief object is to get inside the house, to take off his hat and gloves, and sit at the table punctual to a moment. Depend upon it, the best taste for an approach to a house, is to have it as direct as possible.

The forecourt, unless very ample, was not the place to ramble in leisurely, and make plant to plant visitations. Hollyhocks, dahlias and standard roses were, as a rule, out of taste there—too tall, too straggling, with too much of the rustic about their habit. But he suggests:

For the borders, the very choicest flowering shrubs, such as daphnes, rhododendrons, kalmias, berberies, and dwarf perpetual roses, and the very best herbaceous plants, such as delphiniums, especially the lovely *formosanum*, dielytras [dicentras], antirrhinums, fox-gloves, double Canterbury bells, sweet Williams, wall flowers . . . with fuchsias, pelargoniums, and other greenhouse plants. . . . To support them, and give full effect to their lustre, there should be a wealth of aucubas, hollies, laurels, arbutus, Chinese privet, arbor-vitas, Portugal laurel, Phillyreas, and sweet bays; and for deciduous trees, plane, elm, common and mountain ash, chestnut, thorn, white and green sycamore, purple beech, wild cherry, almond, birch, robinia, lilac, laburnum and lime.

In laying out the garden proper, if you allot a portion to kitchen crops, let it be quite distinct from the flower garden—not mixed up with it. In some suburban gardens, you have to pass rows of cabbages, onions and peas, to get to the beds of roses and the shady arbours.

. . . there is a test by which you may in almost every doubtful case, determine for yourself whether your work is in good taste. Put the question *why?* and let the work give the answer. For instance, you choose a place for a seat—why?—because in that spot there is agreeable shade, and a pretty view; then a seat there placed, is well placed, and not stuck there merely for the sake of having it *somewhere*. Here is a raised bank—why?—to hide a dirty corner where nothing will grow. No, that answer will not do, though it may be literally the truth. . . . Elsewhere you may determine to cut a walk—why?

Leaving 'the green suburbs', we return to 'the close town'.

In an ordinary town garden, measuring, say, some thirty feet by sixty, anything beyond a plain arrangement of oval and circular parterres, separated from the wall borders by a plain continuous path, is out of the question. Some people sketch out a narrow path of the most serpentine outline, which, from a distance, looks like a sandy snake; and this, after leading a visitor from the back door by a number of convolutions over every square yard of the entire garden, until he is dizzy with curves, returning again and again upon themselves, ends abruptly in a high grimy wall, against which a few stones are piled to represent 'rock-work'.

Paths should always be a convenience, *'not a feature'*.

Another person to concern himself with the huge and rising class of ungentlemen was Edward Kemp, Landscape Gardener, of Birkenhead Park. His book *How To Lay Out A Garden: intended as a General Guide in Choosing, Forming, or Improving an Estate (From a Quarter of an Acre to a Hundred Acres in Extent)* was first published in 1850; there was a second edition in 1858 and a third in 1864.

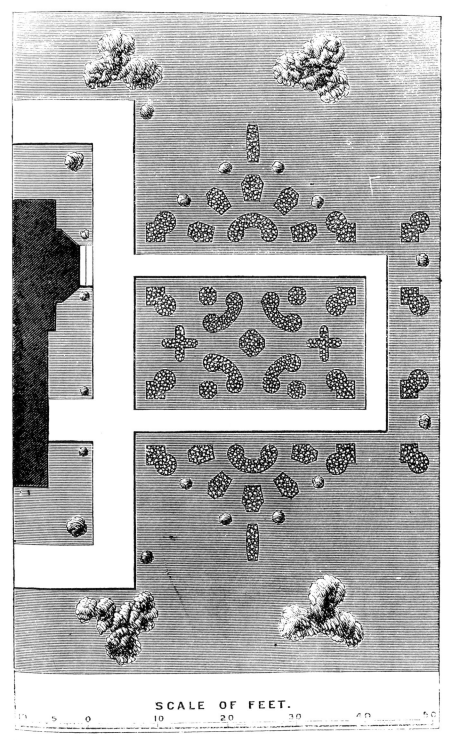

SCALE OF FEET.

15 5 0 10 20 30 40 50

Edward Kemp's plan for Woolton, near Liverpool; another example of drawing board design, from his *How to lay out a Garden* of 1858.

He was an exponent of the Unnatural style, that is to say a mixture of the Geometric and the Picturesque, the Regular and the Irregular, the Clipped and the Unclipped, which was not quite like anything else. His clients resided in Cheshire or Derbyshire, or near Liverpool, or at Kingston in Surrey, Hemel Hempstead, St. Albans and Rickmansworth—places which, with the spread of the railways, could be easily reached from some large town.

He seems to have been a modest man, with excellent intentions, and it is sad to think that his gardens, if one is to judge by the plans he offers, must have been unsatisfactory to look at in almost every way. His style was so entirely typical of what we now think of as a Victorian Garden that it is tempting to think of him as its sole source; while clearly coeval with Paxton and Nesfield, he appears to owe nothing to either of them.

In his Introduction he mentions 'a few valuable hints, which have been mostly acknowledged, gleaned from Sir Uvedale Price, Mr. Repton, and Mr. Loudon. The work of Sir U. Price on "the picturesque", is probably the most valuable thing of the kind in our language. To have collected more from these, or Mr. Gilpin, or any other authority, would have entirely altered the limits and intention of the essay.'

He offers advice on the selection of a site.

A particular locality may, at the time of choosing it, appear highly rural, and have every desirable characteristic; whereas, in a few years, it may become densely covered with small houses or obnoxious manufactories, be cut up into narrow roads, and otherwise be completely spoiled as a place for residence.

His section on 'What to Avoid' tells us a great deal.

Possibly the greatest and most prevalent mistake of those who lay out gardens for themselves is *attempting too much*.

. . . the formation of *numerous flower-beds*, or groups of mixed shrubs and flowers on the lawn. This is a very common failing, and one which greatly disfigures a place; especially as, where intended only for flowers, such beds usually remain vacant and naked for several months in the year.

Later, he suggests growing small evergreen shrubs in pots and sinking them in these flower beds for the winter.

198

At Holmefield, Aigburth, near Liverpool, for Samuel Job, Esq. 1850–51

Andromeda floribunda	Golden Holly
Spiraea Lindleyana	*Cedrus deodara*
Daphne pontica	*Irish Yews*
Hybrid Rhododendron	*Aucuba japonica*
Cotoneaster microphylla	Narrow-leaved Alaternus
Weigela rosea	Double pink Thorn
Tree Ivy	Hodgin's Holly
Weeping Elm	Standard weeping Cherry
Yucca gloriosa	*Cryptomeria japonica*
Yellow-berried Holly	Silver-blotched Holly
Ribes sanguineum	*Ilex marginata*
Ilex balearica	*Pernettya mucronata*
Erica multiflora	*Gaultheria shallon*
Scarlet Thorn	Rhododendron
Variegated prickly Holly	*Araucaria imbricata*
Berberis aquifolium	Double Furze
Ilex Madeirensis	*Cupressus macrocarpa*

Kemp advises against *unnecessary divisions*, as these interrupt 'that beautiful continuity, which does so much in the way of producing size and expression'; against '*a multiplicity of walks*, beyond what are absolutely requisite'; against 'sculptured or other figures, vases, seats, and arbours, baskets for plants', as these will give a small garden 'an affected or ostentatious character'.

Artificial mounds, again, though they may be . . . conducive to effect in certain positions, will, if made too high, or too conspicuous, or too decidedly indicative of art in their formation, be exceedingly unsatisfactory.

Every house must be regarded as a work of art, whatever may be its class or merit; and there would consequently be a want of harmony in associating it with anything composed or resembling the uncultivated parts of nature.

The practice of *planting much immediately around a house* is erroneous. . . . Nothing could be more monotonous than a belt of plantation, in which the trees are nearly all of the same age, height, and general character. . . . Any description of high fence that *confines a place*

Plant Lists from How To Lay Out A Garden *by Edward Kemp, Landscape Gardener, of Birkenhead Park. He seems to have worked principally on acid soils and the shrubs mentioned were generally planted as solitary specimens.*

At Daylesford, Worcestershire, for Harman Grisewood, Esq. 1855:

Half Standard Roses	Laurustinus
Erica carnea	Scarlet Thorn
Irish Yews	*Erica multiflora*
Andromeda floribunda	Clump of mixed dwarf Evergreen
Beds and banks of *Cotoneaster microphylla*	Do of Double Furze
Clusters of mixed *Daphne pontica* and *Berberis aquifolia*	Cluster of Red-flowered Arbutus
Do of Rhododendrons	Portugal Laurel
	Cupressus torulosa
Beds of Hybrid China Roses	*Aucuba japonica*
Bed of mixed Heaths	Tamarisk-leaved Savin
Specimen Rhododendrons	Bed of Ghent Azaleas
Aucuba japonica	*Spiraea Lindleyana*
	Variegated Prickly Holly

too much is as faulty in all essential respects as a belt of plantation. . . . There is an opposite extreme to that just described, into which some persons are apt to fall, by rendering their gardens *too exposed*. . . . The adoption of *too great a mixture of styles* in gardens is an error that should be specially guarded against.

'Unsuitable ornaments, little surprises, and *all manner of eccentricities*' are to be avoided. They are, 'as in personal character, more generally the evidences of a feeble mind, than of the possession of genius. . . . Everything partaking of the nature of a sham', that is to say artificial ruins, mere fronts to buildings, figures to represent animals, bridges for which there is no necessity, 'will be discarded by persons desiring to obtain credit for correct taste.'

Extreme formality or regularity of arrangement, large geometrical figures, very short carriage drives, all are warned against; and, finally, 'kitchen gardens are usually by no means so profitable as they are thought to be. . . . Vegetables can, in most cases, be purchased more cheaply than they can be grown.'

With such a list of prohibitions, one may wonder what the gardens of Edward Kemp actually looked like. In general they had a solemnity which can be accepted, on the one hand, as seriousness of a very high

At Cressbrook, Miller's Dale, Derbyshire, for Henry McConnel, Esq. (no date given)

Large vases, or sculptured figures, on pedestals.

Standard Roses	*Gaultheria procumbens*
Irish Yews, 4 ft. high	*Daphne cneorum*
Fuchsias	*Epigaea repens*
Andromeda floribunda	Beds of Ghent azaleas
Common Laurustinus	Hybrid China Roses
Common Arbutus	good Hybrid Rhododendrons
Irish Yews, 5 ft. high	*Daphne pontica*
Araucaria imbricata	*Aucuba japonica*
Hydrangea hortensis	Double Furze
Cedrus deodara	Cream-coloured Broom
Erica multiflora	*Berberis aquifolium*, with a few of the
Rhododendron hirsutum	dwarfer kinds of Berberry mixed
Gaultheria shallon	Helianthemums
Tamarisk-leaved Savin	Cluster of Hodgin's Holly
Clusters of Common Savin	Beds of mixed evergreen and deciduous
Erica carnea	shrubs

order, or, on the other, as evidence of a total lack of humour. They were made around houses of picturesque outline, in the Tudor Style, the English Gothic Style, the Scotch Style, 'Italian in character', sometimes genuine Elizabethan 'recently extended'.

The house was approached by a curving carriage sweep, but the house itself had most usually a straight terrace immediately next to it. This led, by straight walks, to a parterre of small geometric shapes, either contained by a square of gravel, or a circle, or an octagon, or else just cut out of the lawn. There was a great variety of these shapes, of the kind one might see in a kaleidoscope and, while undoubtedly made with a ruler and compasses, they were certainly unknown to Euclid. They were placed in full view of the house, always to one side.

Beyond this, if there were a beyond, the walks were curving—they did not bend sufficiently often to be called serpentine—decorated with irregular groups of trees or shrubs at regular intervals. Where possible, the property was surrounded by trees, planted on what one might call the Broken Belt System, and which was probably very effective.

The straight walks were bordered with regularly placed small beds, again in a variety of drawing-board shapes. There were many of these, varying from half-circles teamed with whole ones, cricket bails with cricket balls, circles with lozenges, to what one can only call dumbells

William Robinson's Rose Terrace at Gravetye Manor, Sussex.

with holly leaves. They were placed on both sides of the path—occasionally only on one side—and were presumably planted in matching pairs, one bedding-out plant with an edging plant around it. Of clipped shrubs he said:

> . . . instead of fanciful figures or grotesque figures . . . or imitations of animals, the forms should be globular, or pyramidal, or conical, or square, or of any other simple and conventional kind. . . . The sorts of shrub best adapted for this treatment are Yews, Hollies, Box, Portugal Laurel, evergreen Oaks, Phillyreas, Irish Yews, Sweet Bays, hairy Laurustinus, Laurel, Cotoneaster, Taxus adpressa and others.

It was this kind of garden which spread all over the suburbs of England, perhaps as a result of Edward Kemp's book getting into the hands of what he called 'the multitude'. There was a square of lawn with one round bed of geraniums, two clipped holly bushes, a mixed evergreen shrubbery, two urns joined by a balustrade fifteen feet long, and a heap of white stones on one side. It was a recipe for total gloom, but it seems to have been acceptable to a generation that took mourning very seriously.

202

The Wild Revolution

The gardening magazines of the time, which were becoming more and more influential, concentrated increasingly on publicising the new varieties of plant that were now available, with instructions on how to grow them. One of the most successful of these was *Gardening*, later called *Gardening Illustrated*, written principally for the new class of suburban dwellers.

It was owned and edited by William Robinson, who was born of Protestant parents in Ireland in 1838. He was trained there as a working gardener, but by 1861 was in charge of the herbaceous section of the Royal Botanic Society's gardens in Regent's Park. He was particularly attracted by the English wild flowers, of which he made a small collection, and also by the cottage gardens of the English countryside.

By this time, these cottage gardens were collections of sweet herbs, flowers, fruit bushes, fruit trees and vegetables all planted together to no particular plan, but they all had this in common—their owner had a reason for growing them. There was therefore an underlying unity to

Hewell Grange, a Jacobean revival garden of the 1880s.

'Le Style Rothschild', at Ascott in Buckinghamshire, created by Baron Leopold de Rothschild in 1874. At the neighbouring estate of Mentmore, Baron Ferdinand de Rothschild had parrots on stands placed amongst the flower beds, planted so that the flowers matched the birds' feathers.

what could have been no more than a delicious muddle. In general occupying the space between the cottage and the lane, frequently with a hedge with trees growing in it—clipped, or made into standards—it was a kind of gardening precisely suited to the house behind it, and to the countryside in which it lay.

Robinson was a prolific writer and one of his most popular books, *The English Flower Garden*, was first published in 1883. There was a second edition in 1889, but between 1893 and 1905 there were seven more. At the beginning of Chapter III, he said: 'One aim of this book is to uproot the idea that a flower garden must always be of set pattern on one side of the house.'

His idea was to create a wild garden in which 'plants of other countries, as hardy as our hardiest wild flowers' could grow as if they were indeed wild flowers, 'without further care or cost'. His principal target seems to have been Sir Joseph Paxton's garden at the Crystal Palace, made in 1854.

This, in William Robinson's opinion, was 'the fruit of a poor ambition to outdo another ugly extravagance—Versailles'.

His ideas on design were not, in fact, very positive. He knew what he did not like and appeared to suppose that any grouping of plants, in themselves inevitably beautiful, must therefore make a beautiful group. Loudon's opinion had been that even ugly objects, suitably grouped, could be made to look beautiful.

> The first thing is to get a clear idea of the hollowness of much of the talk about 'styles' . . . there are two styles: the one strait-laced, mechanical, with much wall and stone, with fountains and sculpture; the other the natural, which, once free of the house, accepts the ground lines of the earth herself as the best, and gets plant beauty from the flowers and trees arranged in picturesque ways.

> I find it stated by writers on this subject that 'design' can only concern formality. . . . There is more true design in Richmond Park and other noble parks in England, where the trees are grouped in picturesque ways and allowed to take natural forms, than in a French wood with straight lines cut through it, which the first carpenter could design as well as anybody else.

He offers us a plan for the garden of a Tudor house, designed to secure easy cultivation and good effect, and planted with choicest hardy flowers, as one alternative to 'bedding out'.

Above the house, there is a 'Rising slope with groups of flowering shrubs'. These are not specified, but they are contained in shaped beds, rectangles with rounded ends, the shape of an anti-biotic capsule. There is then a trellis of barked oak branches, covered with climbing roses and 'Virgin's Bower' clematis, the wild one, Traveller's Joy. Two flights of steps lead down to a path, presumably gravelled; between them is an immense, straight, sloping border of tea roses carpeted with rockfoils (saxifrages), stonecrops (sedums) and speedwells. At its left is another border of different roses and rockfoil, but with gentians and *Phlox subulata* (a dwarf creeping variety) contained by a stone edging.

On the rectangular lawn—except that, at one corner, it takes a curious dive round a mature yew tree—there are more capsule beds, L-shaped at the corners, planted with more roses and different under-plants. There is a garden of differently sized rectangular beds next to the house, apparently set with crazy paving, planted with roses, roses-and-pansies and carnations. Against an 'Old Wall covered with Erinus alpinus and Fumitory' and climbing roses and clematis, there are two long beds, half-capsules, one with carnations and *Phlox amoena*, the other with carnations and aubrieta, which one can only hope did not flower together.

It is in every way what one must call a 'drawing-board' garden.

> I am a flower gardener, and not a mere spreader about of bad carpets done in reluctant flowers, and when I had a garden of my own to make, I meant it to contain the greatest number of my favourite plants in the simplest way. . . . I did what, so far as we have any evidence to tell us, the Assyrian king and the mediaeval chatelaine did . . . I cut my limited garden space into beds. No plan of any kind was used nor any suggestion sought from any garden. . . . Having made my garden, one day a young lady who had been reading one of those mystifying books about formalities and informalities came in, and, instead of warming her eyes at my roses and carnations, said, 'Oh, you too have a formal garden!' Just imagine what Nebuchadnezzar or the mediaeval lady in their small patches of gardens would think of any silly person who made such a remark instead of looking at the flowers.

In *The Wild Garden*, in its fourth edition in 1894, Robinson concerned himself mostly with plant associations. We find him illustrating 'Double Crimson Paeonies in grass at Crowsley Park', not from a photograph; 'Tiger lilies in the wild garden at Great Tew' and 'Large White Clematis on a yew tree' in the same garden, at one time John Claudius Loudon's. There is also a picture of 'A Beautiful Accident—a colony of *Myrrhis odorata*, in shrubbery not dug, with white Harebells here and there'; of 'A Liane in the North. Aristolochia and Deciduous Cypress'; 'White Climbing Rose scrambling over old Catalpa Tree'; 'A South European Bindweed creeping up the stems of an Iris in an English Garden'; and 'Large White Achilleas, spread into wide masses under shade of trees in shrubbery'.

But oddest of all is in *The English Flower Garden*, where there is an engraving from a photograph of 'A group of house plants placed out for summer' at Harrow Lodge, Dorking. It represents a banana tree, a *Cordyline australis* and three palm trees shivering in a Surrey shrubbery.

Robinson's principal legacy to us must be the naturalising of narcissus and daffodils in grass. This appears to have been something quite new, even in 1894. The commercial growing of these bulbs in fact began in the

1870s, in the Isles of Scilly. Various daffodils growing around Tresco Abbey were hybridised and by 1886 there were 160 varieties to exhibit. By the nineties, therefore, they would have been available in the quantities required for naturalising.

Robinson was for a time joined on *Gardening* by Gertrude Jekyll. Miss Jekyll, who lived to be eighty-nine, was born in 1843, and was thus a contemporary of the French Impressionist painters. She was a gentlewoman, a species only recently extinct, and thus grew up in cultivated surroundings. She became a professional artist but, when her eyesight began to fail, she turned to gardening. She began to design gardens in the 1880s but, as she did not need to work all the time for her living, she was able to devote much of it to the care of what she called 'my little wood of ten acres'.

In the Introduction to *Colour in the Flower Garden*, she says:

To plant and maintain a flower-border, *with a good scheme for colour*, is by no means the easy thing that is commonly supposed.

I am strongly of the opinion that the possession of a quantity of plants, however good the plants may be themselves and however ample their number, does not make a garden; it only makes a *collection*. Having got the plants, the great thing is to use them with careful selection and definite intention. Merely having them, or having them planted unassorted in garden spaces, is only like having a box of paints from the best colourman, or, to go one step further, it is like having portions of these paints set out upon a palette.

Little is known of Miss Jekyll's paintings. It is tempting to suppose that she worked in water-colour, though the previous quotation does not suggest this. Her borders were like Impressionist water-colours, delicate and subtle, each plant placed as Seurat might have placed a spot of colour, not isolated but playing an important part in the whole composition.

In shape, the borders seem to have been long rectangles and she planted them both for colour and for seasonal effect. There were Grey Borders, September Borders and Grey September Borders, for instance. In the Grey Border there were pink hollyhocks, echinops blue, *Achillea* 'Pearl' [pale cream], gypsophila [tiny white flowers] and heliotrope [a soft strong purple] against a background of grey foliage. A detail of the September Border shows perennial asters [michaelmas daisies] and White China Aster 'Mammoth' in front. She seems to have used yellow—which, as

Miss Jekyll was a contributor to William Robinson's magazine, *Gardening Illustrated*. She carried into practice and further developed Robinson's theme of the informal approach. Here, in combination with Sir Edwin Lutyens in his 'grander' manner, she was responsible for the planting at Marsh Court, Hampshire.

every water-colourist knows, is a very dangerous colour—only rarely, and strong reds, very hot blues, scarlets and oranges hardly at all. In plan, her planting can only be called 'abstract'.

Miss Jekyll also naturalised plants. There is a photograph of 'Lilies and Ferns at the Wood Edge near the Lawn' and of 'Polygonum compactum and Megasea [Bergenia] at a Wood Edge'. Her wood was planted to give 'a series of soul-satisfying pictures', each group leading to another like pictures in a gallery. It is her influence which continues to pervade the planting in English Gardens. It would be hard to find, today, a 'serious garden' without at least one herbaceous border planted in her manner, though not necessarily in her taste.

She does not appear to have worked on gardens with William Robinson. Her principal collaborator was Edwin Lutyens, the architect

Tree Peony, Chinese Artist about 1825.

110 Camellias, Augusta Innes Withers 1827.

A hybrid Pelargonium, about 1820.

112 Chrysanthemums, Chinese Artist about 1825.

The new fashionable flowers.

114 *Agrostemma Bungeana.*

113 *Lobelia cardinalis.*

115 *Petunia violacca.*

116 A Gloxinia.

From Paxton's Magazine of Botany.

Park's Yellow Tea-scented China
Redouté.

118 Hume's Blush Tea-scented China
P. J. Redouté.

119 Parson's Pink China   P. J. Redouté.

117–120 *The four China roses from which our modern roses descend.*

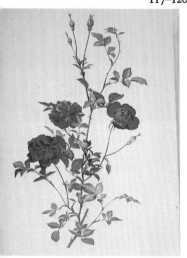

Slater's Crimson China
Willmott.

121 Harrison Weir.

122 Peach Blossom.

Mrs. Harry Turner.

124 Firebrand.

125 Mme. la Baronne de Rothschild.

121–125 Hybrid Perpetual Roses, about 1880.

126 Fuchsias.

127 Chrysanthemums.

128 New Perpetual Carnations.

129 Pompone Dahlias.

Some New Hybrid Flowers, produced between 1878 and 1881.

Lutyens' almost manic concentration on detail shown here in the water garden at Marsh Court.

later to design New Delhi and to be knighted. He did the outline plan and she did the planting, a system still followed today in many local authority offices. The Architects' Department does the plan and the Parks Department does the planting, a possible system only if the two departments are on speaking terms.

One may think that Miss Jekyll might have been wiser to stick to the block planting she so disliked when completing a Lutyens garden. His plans reflected his own overwhelming and individual personality, which must have tended to imprison her softly coloured, gently textured borders, equally individual, but not quite so overwhelming. One of their gardens, at Hestercombe in Somerset, is now in process of a devoted and detailed reconstruction.

*'The lamps are going out all over Europe. We shall not see
them lit again in our lifetime'—Sir Edward Grey*

In about 1906, one of the most influential twentieth-century gardens was
begun at Hidcote Manor in Gloucestershire, by Major Lawrence
Johnston. It was a garden in the tradition of Biddulph Grange, designed
to exclude the countryside—not to take into account the genius of the
place—and to provide shelter for an immense collection of plants from all
over the world. He reverted, in some ways, to the late seventeenth
century, planting alleys, and making compartments, of clipped yew and
hornbeam, and these were decorated with informal, or abstract plantings,
rather in the manner of Gertrude Jekyll. There was a Yellow Garden,
some Red Borders, an alley of pleached hornbeam, a Dell Garden, a
Topiary Garden with shrub roses, a Rock Garden, a Pool Garden and a
calm, open space.

At the same time Mr. Herbert Goode, a wealthy china and glass
merchant, started a Japanese Garden not far from Cambridge. It was
designed by a Japanese landscape architect, brought over for the purpose,
and the garden furniture, the houses, the bridges and gateways, were
made in Japan. It was surrounded by an Italian Garden and was, and is, a
most beautiful example of Japanese garden making. At the same time, it

An early plan of
Hidcote Manor
Gardens in 1913.
Lawrence Johnston
started developing the
hillside site on the edge
of the Cotswolds in
1906. It was planted by
him over the next
thirty years to make
one of the most
admired of 20th-
century gardens.

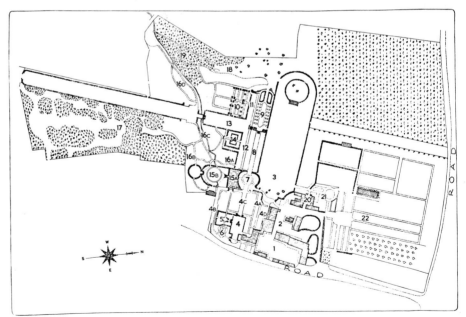

210

The armaments manufacturer, William Armstrong, brought a barren moorland hillside under control. Cragside, begun in 1863, has matured into a great garden. Norman Shaw—the architect—rose to the challenge of the site and produced a suitably eccentric masterpiece.

must represent the height of the movement away from making English Gardens in England. The vogue for Japanese Gardens continued for some years, though frequently some water, a few irises and some concrete temple lanterns were considered sufficient to brand a garden as Japanese. The rage for autumn colour also began about this time, prompted partly by the fact that members of the Maple family, both American and Japanese, were now much more readily available.

In Northumberland, at Cragside, a large tract of moorland had been planted in the 1870s with Canadian conifers, rhododendrons, berberis and gaultheria which gradually took over the whole area. Today one can see whole hillsides on which there is not a single native plant.

At Iford Manor, in Wiltshire, at about the beginning of this century, an Italian garden was made by its owner, Harold Peto. The hill above and behind the house was terraced and various real Italian objects, including a monastery cloister, were imported. Planted with roses, rosemary and lavender, among many other kinds of plant, it sought to re-create not Classical or Mediaeval Italy, but the Italy of the time, of Rimini, Rapallo and Max Beerbohm.

Whatever their style, the gardens of this time all had one thing in common. They required an immense amount of maintenance. In this connection, mention must be made of Miss Ellen Willmott, whose book *The Genus Rosa* must have done much to wean people away from the barmaid roses of the late nineteenth century, superb though many of them were, towards the ramblers and shrub roses of the early twentieth.

At her garden at Warley Place, near Brentwood in Essex, eighty-six gardeners looked after a rock garden of three acres, herbaceous borders, rose gardens, a large water and bog garden, orchid and palm houses, propagating houses for alpine and other plants, a huge kitchen and fruit garden and a considerable range of greenhouses. Her contribution to horticulture was enormous, commemorated by various plants called Miss Willmott, Warleyensis or Willmottianum, but her garden was doomed to disappear.

With the outbreak of war in 1914, the twentieth century began in earnest.

Opposite and above: Harold Peto's own garden at Iford Manor in Wiltshire. Peto, who worked mostly in the south of France, brought back to his own garden architectural features that he had acquired in France and Italy. Both amateur and professional garden designers have been notorious for not knowing where to stop and Peto was a classic example. The multiplicity of garden ornament at Iford bears this out.

Scale of Feet.   60   48   36   2+   12   0   6   12

a to *b*. Arcade of trellis work.   No. 3.   *c. c.* Covered Seats.

Garden design on the drawing board—a plan of a Rose Garden by William Paul 1880.

PART SEVEN

Technicolor and Technology,
1914-1979

Garden design by Percy Cane about 1930.

Above and opposite top: Anglesey Abbey, near Cambridge, begun by Lord Fairhaven in 1930 in open fields. It is planted with a number of avenues which, sadly, lead nowhere in particular. Also, a great deal of statuary is scattered around the garden.

'I know the names of more plants than you do'

Gardening now became more and more a question of which plant to put where. If there were a question of style, then in general the past was consulted, but not too closely. One of the largest gardens made in the nineteen-thirties, at Anglesey Abbey near Cambridge, seems to have used the early eighteenth century as its model. But, by using plants which that century did not use, the impression given is not so much of an imitation as of a rather careless copy.

Achille Duchêne's formal water garden at Blenheim. Duchêne restored many of the famous Châteaux gardens in France at the turn of the century. He began work at Blenheim in 1908 and finished the water garden in 1930.

Rex Whistler's *trompe l'oeil* plan of Sir Philip Sassoon's garden at Port Lympne in Kent, 1930. The garden was begun by Sir Philip in 1912.

At Port Lympne, near Folkestone, a remarkable terraced garden was completed at this time. Made on a hillside overlooking Romney Marsh, the house was halfway down the hill, surrounded by small gardens planted in an original way, a checkerboard garden, for instance, and a marigold garden in simple stripes of one colour. There were also some spectacular borders planted in blocks. But a principal feature was a magnificent set of stone steps, with terraces leading off them to individual gardens planted for their colour. These unfortunately did not really lead anywhere; at the top, one had to turn round and come down again. A plan of the original garden was painted on a wall of the house by Rex Whistler and it is being carefully and lovingly restored by its present owner.

218

Above: The Marigold Garden at Port Lympne in 1933, planted with dahlias.

Below: The fountain pool overlooking Romney Marsh. This has now been altered, but the new owners are sympathetically restoring much of the original garden.

Sir John Ramsden created the great curving terrace at Muncaster Castle in Cumbria in 1918. Here the scale is magnificent. This huge terrace is backed by small trees and shrubs and not by a belt of forest trees as at Rievaulx.

At Sissinghurst Castle, also in Kent, a garden was begun in 1930 which, with its formal shapes and informal plantings, must remain a perfect example of the gardens of the time. Made on the site, and indeed over the bones of, a Tudor castle, its shape was necessarily compartmented. Old walls were retained, yew hedges were planted, by V. Sackville-West to the design of her husband, Harold Nicolson.

She can be said to have followed Gertrude Jekyll in her use of colour groupings: a purple border, a cottage garden in red, orange and yellow, a walled garden devoted to nineteenth-century roses, pink, purple, white and striped, underplanted with lavender, pinks and irises, a white garden, a herb garden. She was for many years the gardening correspondent of the *Observer* and the distinction of her taste permeated, by this means, the gardening world of the nineteen-fifties and early 'sixties.

At the height of its glory, her garden had all the unselfconscious charm which only art, love and knowledge combined can produce. There was no regimentation; nothing was forced. The impression given was that every plant in the garden was delighted to be there. She chose them because she loved them; and, perhaps, they knew that.

Elsewhere, the trend was firmly inwards. The large suburban garden and the small country garden approached one another both in form and content. The focus of these gardens was the grass tennis court, made at no matter what cost to the rest of the garden. There was a double border; a group of flowering trees (*floribundissima semperflorens*); some nice beds, preferably sunk, surrounded with crazy paving and filled with hybrid tea roses which were not underplanted; some kind of terrace from which to watch the tennis; a garden house for the croquet mallets and the spare tennis net; a shrubbery; a goldfish pond—certainly sunk—surrounded with crazy paving; a rock garden with a gnome or two; and a number of little pots each containing, in the summer, one geranium.

The motor mower, like the motor car, was by now well within the reach of the owners of such houses, whose children now began to meet socially and, sometimes, to marry. 'Going Round the Garden' became a subject for revue sketches, the host determined to find at least one plant whose name his guest did not know, the guest contenting himself—or more usually herself—with counting the weeds and those tell-tale little black spots on the rose leaves.

Flower hybridisation continued apace. The delphinium grew taller and taller, requiring more and more staking; the dahlia grew larger and larger, requiring more and more staking; the gladiolus assumed its present martial proportions and the rose its present scentless glory. It would not be

The Old Fashioned Rose Garden in the Nicolsons' famous garden at Sissinghurst Castle, in Kent, photographed in the 1950s. Due to the enormous number of visitors this garden attracts each year, it has had to be 'tidied up' and has lost its cornucopia-like magic.

quite true to say that the Scentless Rose was the great achievement of the nineteen-thirties, since it might be hard to discover exactly when the first scentless rose was produced; but rose breeding moved away from the soft colourings of even the previous decade towards the hot yellows, blood reds and sharp oranges of the present day.

In 1925, Mrs. Reis began replanting a 1900-garden. Tintinhull in Somerset, with Hidcote and Sissinghurst, set a fashion in garden design which has lasted to the present day. Within a formal framework of hedges, walls and pleached alleys, separate small gardens were created.

Hardly the place for dwarf Irises

Shortly after her marriage to Lord Ridley in 1924, Ursula, the second daughter of Edwin Lutyens, wished to make some changes in the Quarry Garden at Blagdon.

On the back of a large mounted photograph she wrote, to Gertrude Jekyll: '*General view of quarry, on entering over bridge in SE angle—showing sycamore in centre.*'

Returning the photograph, and sending a plan, Miss Jekyll observed: 'The grassy spaces south of this are what I think should be kept clear & quiet—I should even be inclined to have something shrubby enough on the Sycamore side of the slight mound (5 in my plan) to hide the flowers beyond when approaching from the South.'

The correspondence continued in this way. The second photograph was '*looking straight at bridge of access S.E.*'.

Miss Jekyll remarked: 'Here and all round and about the big sycamore in the middle space I think should be kept as quiet grassy spaces, the better to lead to the flowery parts beyond.'

Photograph 3: '*Showing sycamore and wellingtonia on extreme right—the latter ought to come down.*'

'Yes, Wellingtonia should come away—some Hollies would be right backing the fine Sycamore. Here also the grass should be kept quiet except perhaps for some Daffodils? I mean no additions of flowering trees or bushes.'

'*Yes. I think some daffodils wd. look well here. The two little maples marked X are green not the red kind—you have shifted them in the plan—but they look alright there—or wd. you have them away altogether? The Wellingtonia is down, and it is a great improvement.*'

Photograph 4: '*Showing same trees as in No. 3 and part of stone bridge over stream.*'

'Same remarks as on 3. In the small photographs first sent that invading polygonum showed up rather finely against the dark of one of these arches & might be retained unless you are against it altogether. There is a better kind P. molle that is really a beautiful thing that should suit the place well. It is also something of an invader but not so bad a one as your cleaned out Sieboldii.'

'*The polygonum is still against the bridge and I am all for leaving it. It is fun to have some, as children love it so.*'

Photograph 5: '*Showing good holly and another Wellingtonia (doomed!)*'

'Yes, the Wellingtonia should certainly go. I take it that this is the upper part of the region where I should advise a good planting of Daffodils in the grass.'

'*What I have called the Wellingtonia is really a Deodar Cedar. I see you have it marked on the plan as a cedar of Lebanon and have done some planting accordingly. I have taken it away as it was a poor tree, and looks much better away. It leaves a good corner for planting shrubs. I think you have suggested planting rather too many hollies here on the plan. I feel one wants to get as much colour here as possible, and suggest shrubs like the blue ceanothus or orange budleia wd. look well against the grey bridge. What do you think?*'

'Yes. Ceanothus best. G.J.'

Photograph 6: '*Showing face of wall very suitable for wistaria or climbing rose etc. (Rubbish heap in centre foreground has since been burnt).*'

'This looks like the place for the main moraine which seems to be there already just under that pretty little tree that hangs down and clutches hold by the root. The wooded top looks to want more planting on the left (above the Irish yews & towards the middle). Birch and green Holly here again would be excellent & one or two Rambling Roses swinging about but only those of the wildish sort. Another capital thing for this sort of use is the wild Clematis Vitalba.

Wistaria would be pretty but is very slow to grow.

The moraine here would be a good place for gentian & some of the green-leaved mossy saxifrages.'

'*There is no moraine in the corner at present—but it would be a good place to make one. On the plan you have planted this corner with Aesculus. It wd. be a splendid place for Clematis & roses. Could you give me the names of the best rambling roses? Clematis montana would look lovely besides Vitalba?*'

'Rose Evangeline best of all—a lovely thing like a much larger pinkish dogrose.'

Photograph 7: '*Showing weeping elm—we need along the top to clear out conifers & plant forest trees (silver birch?). There are some very pretty maples behind the weeping elm—the messy shrubs to the left of this have been cleared away.*'

'Yes—silver birch by all means & hollies at the back of them—there is nothing to beat this combination.'

'*I see you have this weeping elm marked on the plan as a snowy mispulus, & have done some planting accordingly. Would you still do the same planting? There is a mass of primroses under the tree & some daffodils round it already there.*'

'It was not my mistake this time, as it is already marked snowy mespilus on your original plan & I was puzzled because it did not look like one in this picture also I could not account for a weeping elm elsewhere.'

Photograph 8: '*Showing face of wall very suitable for any small rock plants. Would you let the ivy grow again on the bank on the top of the wall—where the earth is now rather bare?*'

'Certainly a place for some rock plants. Pile up the natural stones into a sort of small moraine—a ground work of the natural soil & grit; the stones half buried, but all pointing one way as if they had slithered down. Don't abolish the ivy altogether but let it grow moderately; partly veiling the top edge of the cliff.'

'*I am clearing a lot of saplings away from the top of the cliff to make room for the laburnam.*'

Photograph 9: '*Bits of this cliff are very damp—one might plant dwarf irises in the shelves & crevices.*'

'Hardly the place for dwarf irises. Better for some of the good saxifrages, S. umbrosum (London Pride) perhaps best of all, or some of the white plumed kinds such as S. pyrimidalis, S. longifolia, S. cotyledon, these are some of the white

Munstead Wood. Photograph by
Gertrude Jekyll, 1900.

The Japanese Garden at Cottered.

132 (*Above*) Hidcote and 133 (*Below*) Nymans.

134 (*Top*) and 135 (*Bottom*) Port Lympne in the 1930s.

136 (*Top*) Wisley.

137 (*Left*) 'The Japanese Garden' at Compton Acres.

138 (*Below*) The first garden gnome.

Sheffield Park, Sussex. Originally by Brown, followed by Repton, it is now a woodland garden.

plume flowering kinds. There is also a beautiful short growing kind with white flowers S. Wallacia.

This would also bear a little moraine in that middle cavity.

The ivy is very good here—just right. Also at the foot of the scarp some of the mossy saxifrages would do well—S. Decopius with red flowers and S. Muscoides with white flowers.'

Photograph 10: '*It is very damp under this arch. Those are cherries growing under the arch—& Wellingtonia is to come down.*'

'Just behind where the Wellingtonia now stands a biggish group of the fine Spiraea Aruncus would be fine, & in front of it a drift of Iris (purple) sibirica & in the grass or rough ground in front a bold planting of the large purple cranesbill (Geranium Ibericum).'

'*I love this idea, but you have put Pyrus Malus on the plan just here—which would be best? I think this idea on the whole.*'

'Yes, the planting as overleaf will be better here than the Pyrus Malus—it was my mistake. I had not clearly made out the plan.'

Photograph 11: '*Just showing steps up & out of quarry. Suitable bank on left for primroses or any low growing plant.*'

'There are plants that would be better here than primroses—drifts of fritillary (Fritillaria meleagris) for spring & colchicum autumnale for autumn.'

The Quarry Garden is now planted with a handsome collection of maples.

Ditchley Park in Oxfordshire. A formal garden by Geoffrey Jellicoe made in the 1930s.
Only the pleached hornbeams and hedges now remain.

In the ribbon development houses of the time, often on the Elizabethan
cottage model, the mode was for crazy paving, dwarf conifers, weeping
trees, gnomes and other tiny ornaments, sundials, very small ponds and
rockeries. To use a word of the time, they were 'twee'.

The great Edwardian gardens, already beginning to gasp for lack of
labour, began to disappear behind dense plantations of rhododendrons,
azaleas and camellias. Where the soil was right, whole gardens were
devoted to these; and where the soil was not right it was changed, by
advancing technology, so that a hillside of heather could be planted, for
instance, near Stow-on-the-Wold. The fashion for maples continued; the
passion for autumn colour spread to the herbaceous border.

No style of gardening arose to complement the Art Deco house, or
those houses and blocks of flats whose windows go round corners and
which appear, in profile, to be gnashing their teeth. The half-sunburst, a
favourite motif of the time, appearing on gates, fire-screens, cinema
curtains and wirelesses, would in fact have been an ideal plan for a front
garden.

Bentley's, near Halland in Sussex. A very simple terrace garden designed by Christopher Tunnard and Serge Chermayeff in 1937.

In 1937, at Bentley's in Sussex, the architect Serge Chermayeff built a house for himself in an advanced contemporary style, and set it in a simple landscape of grass and trees. His example has since been followed, not always wisely, by local authorities, who have discovered, just as Lancelot Brown did, that Grass-and-Trees require less maintenance than any other kind of garden.

The terrace at Bentley's. The plinth at the far end of the terrace was to have a reclining figure by Henry Moore. This has gone and a lot of recent gardening has appeared.

Blagdon in Northumberland. Lutyens designed the formal canal in 1939.

In 1939, at Blagdon in Northumberland, the architect Sir Edwin Lutyens completed, at his daughter's house, a belvedere and the Long Water, an early-eighteenth century canal with a false perspective at the end. It was to be almost the last piece of garden layout on the grand scale.

What nearly all these gardens had in common was the desire to exclude. This had in fact been the tendency since Loudon, but it now became the object of many garden makers, to exclude the view (if they were lucky enough to have one), to exclude the world, the office and those horrid people next door, and to create a world of its own which was safe, secure and secret.

'Take it from us, it is utterly forbidden to be half-hearted about Gardening. You have got to LOVE your garden, whether you like it or not'—W. C. Sellar and R. J. Yeatman, Garden Rubbish, *1936*

The Second World War almost put an end to the professional gardener as a species. He continued in nurseries and in the public parks, but only very rarely in private employment.

Faced with this problem, his previous employers sold the tennis court—which had been dug up for vegetables anyway during the war—and planted a hedge of *Cupressocyparis leylandii* to screen them from the house that was immediately built upon it. Fortunately, the dwarf conifers which they had bought fifteen years ago—they couldn't quite remember where—were now so colossal that they screened them from the instant house that was being built on what had been the vegetable garden.

Then they closed down one of the double borders and planted some rhododendrons in little round peat beds—as the soil wasn't quite right—where it had been. Then they filled the goldfish pond with what had been the rockery and planted a birch tree on top of it. The terrace was beginning to get rather the worse for wear, but they couldn't find anyone to re-point it, so they filled the holes with aubrieta, dwarf pinks, helianthemums and irises and then they found they couldn't use it as they were always tripping up. Also it seemed to make such a lot of work. Luckily, the aubrieta soon took it over.

The hedge of *Cupressocyparis leylandii* was now so tall that it excluded all the sun from the remaining herbaceous border so they ripped it up and put it down to shrubs, not those dreary old Victorian ones but *variegated* shrubs, underplanted with gold and grey-leaved little plants and punctuated by a few more dwarf conifers. They also planted some flowering cherry trees, birches and laburnums at the bottom of the garden to screen them from the nasty council estate that was rising where old Mrs.

A number of post-war gardens have been created in the tradition of Hidcote, Tintinhull and Sissinghurst, all looking to the past for inspiration. John Fowler's own garden, near Odiham, was begun in 1947. Hornbeam hedges and pleached hornbeams set off the Hunting Lodge, an 18th century Gothick folly.

229

View from the Hunting Lodge towards the lake.

Whatsit used to live. They underplanted them with camellias in little round peat beds, because the soil wasn't quite right. Then they sold.

The new owner, happily, was a frightfully keen gardener, so the first thing he did was to completely re-do the front garden, until then just a bit of grass. He designed a charming wavy path made of crazy paving which wound around in a very cunning way, and planted the spaces with creeping dwarf conifers and a lot of upright dwarf conifers, quite a lot of dwarf maples and a great many dwarf variegated shrubs. Then he found some gnomes in an old shed behind a laurel bush, which was full of rotting tennis nets, so he put them among the creeping conifers where nobody could see them anyway because of the enormous ilex tree which occupied the whole of the bit along the road, recently adopted by the council. Fortunately, the council told him to cut it down as they were afraid its roots might one day disturb the pavement they had just laid over its roots. So he was able to plant a hedge of *Cupressocyparis leylandii* at the front as well.

He discovered that what he had thought was a sort of rock garden was really a terrace so he dug all the plants up and had it concreted, made a barbecue at one end and a patio garden at the other, with a sort of home extension over it, and on that he planted a Russian vine. Then he went to

230

Chelsea and saw a marvellous exhibit in which everything was growing in 'island beds'. So he carved up the whole of his garden into a series of weird, jig-saw puzzle shapes, islands, peninsulas, promontories *and* isthmuses. He put down a lot of peat and then—as it was July by this time—was lucky enough to find a Garden Centre which had everything in containers.

So he was able to plant more rhododendrons, more camellias, quite a lot of that evergreen viburnum, juniper, thuya, *Cupressus lawsoniana*, some nice big heathers, a lot of berberis as ground cover, a contorted willow, some forsythias, a fatsia or two, a weeping flowering cherry, some small heathers, a purple weeping birch, a weeping beech, a silver pear, some purple sycamores, four mountain ashes and a whitebeam. Then he noticed that the Russian vine was taking the roof off so he, too, sold.

The new owner was not a gardener. He made a lovely bright blue swimming pool (himself) which exactly followed the amoeboid outline of one of his predecessor's island beds, concreted the rest and lived happily ever after.

A camel is a horse designed by a committee

One of the great sadnesses of the moment must be the performance of the public authorities in the gardening department. They have more power than the eighteenth-century landowner ever dreamed of; and an earth-moving technology that the nineteenth century only guessed at.

It was not to be expected that the industrial working class, released at last from its formidable slums, would instantly formulate an excellent plan for a working class garden. A quiet reversion to the cottage garden of the nineteenth century would have exactly suited them, but by this time many of them had hardly even a great-grandparent born in the countryside.

Herded into desolate new towns, overwhelmed by regulations which touched even their gardens, a feeling of discouragement was bound to follow. Filed firmly away in concrete tower blocks, even window-box gardening turned out to be nearly impossible on the windswept upper

Miles Hadfield's reconstruction of a knot garden made in 1640, in its turn an adaptation of a design which appeared in *The Gardener's Labyrinth*. This photograph was taken just after work started in 1960, at Moseley Old Hall.

storeys—one thing every plant dislikes is wind. The ground below them could have been made into parks for walking in, playgrounds for playing in, scented flower gardens for older people to sit in; but this did not happen.

It would be hard to imagine a garden less jubilant, or less like a garden, than the Jubilee Garden on the South Bank in London; or anything more eccentric and unsuitable than the 'Victorian' and 'Elizabethan' gardens made round the beautiful, defenceless Elizabethan house at Temple Newsam by the Leisure Committee of the Leeds City Council. One receives the impression that each member of this Committee—all, one feels sure, keen amateur gardeners—was given a portion of graph paper on which to delineate their thoughts and that these were then stuck haphazardly together, as in a game of 'Consequences'.

No style of gardening, or landscaping, has appeared to mitigate the horrors of the New Brutalism in architecture. At the London Concrete Culture Complex, acres of municipal paving are deemed to be sufficient, punctuated occasionally by sad plane trees dropped into holes in the pavement, where they mourn to a slow death. Round some of the larger London council housing projects a passion for little bumps has manifested

Russell Page designed this garden for Lady Caroline Somerset at Badminton, in the 1950s.

itself, presumably 'diversifying' the flatness of the ground, but in fact looking like so many mass graves. These grassy areas are mostly dedicated to the well-known pastime of 'No Ball Games'.

Parks and gardens must be thought of, initially, in terms of plants. It is about as sensible to assume that architects can automatically design gardens as it is to suppose that a sculptor can also write symphonies. The idea that any two local authority departments are going to combine to produce the harmonious whole that parks and gardens ought to be is too frivolous to be entertained for a second. All that the Jubilee Garden does is to demonstrate, *most* expensively, the state of the Disunited Kingdom in 1977.

In the private garden, if our gardens are complacent, conformist and compartmented, with timid lines and greedy planting ('There *must* be somewhere for it—the Joneses have got one'), then they are doing no more than reflect the society that has emerged since the war. If many gardeners suppose that, if they concentrate sufficiently fiercely on the details, some fine overall pattern is bound to appear, they are doing no more than follow the deepest thoughts of their political leaders.

If the new garden owner expects to have a garden in full bloom from January to December, mature from the moment it is planted, maintained with no effort from himself and at no cost, it is no more than a sign of the almost total divorce of the English people today from the soil. To many people, the countryside is nothing more than a huge park without any litter baskets.

If the English have a fault—and it is possible to think this—it is a tendency to overdo everything, to over-administer, to over-regulate, to over-protect, to put too many ingredients in their food, too much furniture in their rooms and to use too many colours practically everywhere. There is also a tendency to put far too many plants in their gardens.

The sad thing is, of course, that gardening is an art. Artists of all kinds are rare and, in this country at least, notably uncherished and unsought. Artists in the garden are perhaps the rarest of all, so complicated is it as a medium. There must be a feeling for the plants, as well as a knowledge of them. There must be an ability to accept the limitations of the ground, wherever it may be, and an ability to select the plants that will like to grow in the available soil and with the available aspect. It is often forgotten that plants are alive and there is, as yet, no Society for the Prevention of Cruelty to them.

So where, you seem to be saying, do we go from here?
Well.
Here is a pronouncement of authority, from the British Standards Institution's Code of Practice, CP2004, 1972.

> Buildings with foundations not more than 1 m (3 ft) deep on shrinkable clays should be kept at a distance from all trees of at least the mature height of the tree; if the trees are in rows, the distance should be increased. This rule should also be observed for trees planted after the building is completed. Shrubs may also cause damage to shallow foundations.

In other words, if your tree is going to grow to forty feet, it must be planted forty feet away from your foundations. Street planting—except, of course, with dwarf conifers—would thus become impossible. Grass, too, can dry the soil to a depth of five feet, causing shrinkage. If trees, and grass, and shrubs, are to be restricted, gradually—such is the nature of the English—all forms of green life will be restricted. The planned garden will be made of concrete.

All the oxygen in the air is made by plants.
Even bureaucrats need oxygen.

No Ball Games.
No Ball Games On Grass Verges.

No grass verges?

It will be interesting to see what happens.

POSTSCRIPT

'A legal right the proprietor unquestionably has to deform his ruin, as he pleases. But tho' he fear no indictment in the king's bench, he must expect a very severe prosecution in the court of taste.' Thus the Reverend William Gilpin on the resuscitation of Fountains Abbey, furiously remarking that *restoration* was apparently not enough, that *ornaments* had to be added. His comments on ruins apply exactly to the restoration of gardens today.

The 'ornaments' most commonly added to defenceless 'period' gardens considered ripe for preservation are, of course, random flower beds and haphazard flowering shrubs, introduced under the impression that what the public *really* likes is a nice bit of colour. Colour is, in any case, extremely difficult to use well. One must go to the Impressionist painters, to the Chinese ceramicists, to the makers of Persian rugs, of Indian and Siamese fabrics, to learn how to use colour in the garden. It ought not to be entrusted to people who are, in Sir William Chambers' words, 'well skilled in the culture of sallads, but little acquainted with the principles of Ornamental Gardening'.

A good garden needs no gift-wrapping. If it was originally conceived in terms of one colour—green—and the principal interest given by the constant interplay of leaf texture, then to 'liven it up' with a few beds of geraniums is as pointless and as tasteless as the sticking of loud posters all over Westminster Abbey 'to bring the people in'.

The authentic flavour of a garden can be preserved only by using in it plants that *could have been* planted in it when it was first made. There can be no point in laying out a Tudor Knot Garden, even from a contemporary plan, if the knots are carried out only in box and the interstices filled with the latest annual hybrids; it will merely demonstrate the ignorance of the people concerned. There can be no point in covering genuine late seventeenth-century terraces with a creeping carpet of herbaceous plants, not one of which was known in this country when the terraces were made; it will merely detract from their dignity. There can be absolutely no point in replacing a native tree with a suburban flowering tree because it is such a picture for a fortnight in the spring; the scale will be entirely different and there are twenty-six fortnights in the year.

Our ancestors were extremely clever at suiting their materials to their purpose. If we wish to preserve their work, we must consult their taste and their intentions. There is no reason to suppose that their ignorance was as colossal as our arrogance, that they knew nothing about anything because their contemporaries were unable to walk on the moon. They were closer to the soil, and to reality, than we are. Their wisdom was acquired by experience and it is foolish to ignore it.

We have tried to show some of the results of their wisdom and their experience in the garden. As John James said, all those years ago: 'It costs no more to execute a good Design, than an ill one!'

P O M O N A

Appendix One

A Chronological List of Gardens, Gardeners and Authors mentioned in this book.

(The most important and influential are given in capital letters. Where a garden was the creation of its owner, the name of the garden is given first. Works of literature are given in italics. A selection of the works of Bridgeman, Kent, Brown and Repton is given at Appendix Two)

John Evelyn

Henry Wise

c. 1440	*The Feate of Gardening*, by Mayster John Gardener
1557	*Hundreth Good Pointes of Husbandrie*, by Thomas Tusser
1576	Isaac de Caus born (died 1626). Garden at Wilton House, Wiltshire
1586	*The Gardener's Labyrinth*, by Didymus Mountain, otherwise Thomas Hill
c. 1590	Claude Mollet gardener at Les Tuileries, Paris
1606	EDMUND WALLER born (died 1687). Poet. Own garden at Hall Barn, Beaconsfield
1613	*The English Husbandman*, by Gervase Markham
1614	*Cheap and Good Husbandry*, by Gervase Markham
1618	*A New Orchard and Garden*, by William Lawson
1620	JOHN EVELYN born (died 1706). Own gardens at Sayes Court, Deptford, and Wotton, Surrey Andre Mollet, son of Claude, summoned to England from France
1621	*The Anatomy of Melancholy*, by Robert Burton Oxford Physic Garden founded
1625	*Of Gardens*, by Sir Francis Bacon
1628	SIR WILLIAM TEMPLE born (died 1699). Own garden at Moor Park, Surrey
1629	JOHN ROSE born (died 1677). Royal Gardener at St. James's Park *Paradisus in Sole*, by John Parkinson

c. 1640	GEORGE LONDON born (died 1713).	Royal Gardeners to Queen Anne. Worked at Longleat, Hampton Court, Windsor, Blenheim Palace, Melbourne Hall
1653	HENRY WISE born (died 1738).	

1661	Andre Mollet, with his nephew Gabriel, Royal Gardeners in St. James's Park
1664	SIR JOHN VANBRUGH born (died 1726). Architect and Playwright. Temple and HaHas at Castle Howard and Duncombe Park, Yorkshire. Castle at Claremont, Surrey *Sylva, A Discourse of Forest Trees*, by John Evelyn
1665	*Flora, Ceres and Pomona*, by John Rea gent (1st edition)
1670	*The English Gardner*, by Leonard Meager (1st edition)
1672	JOHN JAMES born (died 1746). Architect. Own garden at Warbrook, Hampshire

238

1680   CHARLES BRIDGEMAN born (died 1738). Landscape Gardener (see Appendix Two)

1682   STEPHEN SWITZER born (died 1745). Landscape Gardener and Seedsman. Garden at Grimsthorpe, Yorkshire

1683   *Systema Horticultura, or The Art of Gardening*, by J. W. Gent otherwise John Worlidge

1685   WILLIAM KENT born (died 1748). Architect and Landscape Gardener (see Appendix Two)

1688   ALEXANDER POPE born (died 1744). Poet. Own garden at Twickenham, Middlesex

c. 1690   Celia Fiennes rode through England on a side-saddle

1690   Garden at Levens Hall, Cumbria, begun by Monsieur Beaumont for Sir James Grahame

Charles Bridgeman

1694   LORD BURLINGTON born (died 1733). Kent's patron. Own garden at Chiswick House

1695   Garden at Inkpen Old Rectory, Berkshire, begun

1696   Garden at Melbourne Hall, Derbyshire, begun by London & Wise for Thomas Coke

c. 1700   Terraces at Powys Castle begun by Lord Rockford and Lord Powys

1712   *The Theory and Practice of Gardening*, translated from the French, by John James Terrace at Duncombe Park begun by Thomas Duncombe I

1715   *An Essay on Criticism*, by Alexander Pope
LANCELOT BROWN born (died 1783). Landscape Gardener (see Appendix Two)

c. 1715   Garden at Studley Royal begun by John Aislabie

1717   SANDERSON MILLER born (died 1780). Gentleman Architect and Gardener. Terrace at Farnborough Hall, Oxfordshire. Garden at Wimpole, Cambs. Own garden at Radway Grange, Warwickshire

William Kent

1718   Garden at Ebberston Hall, Yorkshire, begun by William Thompson
The Nobleman, Gentleman and Gardener's Recreation, by Stephen Switzer

1720   Garden at St. Paul's, Walden Bury, Hertfordshire, begun by Edward Gilbert

1724   *Tour through the Whole of England and Wales*, by Daniel Defoe

1726   SIR WILLIAM CHAMBERS born (died 1796). Architect. Buildings and Garden at Kew, Surrey. Village of Milton Abbas, Dorset, with Lancelot Brown

1728   *The New Principles of Gardening*, by Batty Langley of Twickenham

1730   *The Seasons*, a poem by James Thomson

1735   *Ferme Ornée* at Woburn Farm, Surrey, begun by Philip Southcote

1741   Henry Hoare inherited Stourhead, Wiltshire

1743   Garden at The Leasowes, near Halesowen, Shropshire, begun by William Shenstone

1745   Garden at Pains Hill, Surrey, begun by the Hon. Charles Hamilton
Ruined Castle at Hagley, Worcestershire, by Sanderson Miller for Lord Cobham

1747   UVEDALE PRICE born (died 1829). Own garden at Foxley, Herefordshire

Capability Brown

Richard Payne Knight

Humphry Repton

John Claudius Loudon

1750 RICHARD PAYNE KNIGHT born (died 1824). Own garden at Downton Castle, Herefordshire
Terrace at Rievaulx, Yorkshire, begun by Thomas Duncombe III

1752 HUMPHRY REPTON born (died 1818). Landscape Gardener (see Appendix Two)

1757 *Designs of Chinese Buildings*, by Sir William Chambers

c. 1765 *Observations on Modern Gardening*, by Thomas Whately

1772 The Reverend William Gilpin made his tour of England
A Dissertation on Oriental Gardening, by Sir William Chambers

1783 JOHN CLAUDIUS LOUDON born (died 1843). Edited the first gardening magazine. Own gardens at Great Tew, Oxfordshire, and Porchester Terrace, Bayswater

1785 *Essay on Modern Gardening*, by Horace Walpole

1793 WILLIAM NESFIELD born (died 1881). Engineer and Gardener. Gardens at Broughton, Yorkshire; Harewood, Yorkshire; Holkham, Norfolk; Castle Howard, Yorkshire; Witley Court, Worcestershire; Kew

1794 *Essays on the Picturesque*, by Uvedale Price
An Analytical Enquiry into the Principles of Taste, by Richard Payne Knight

1795 SIR CHARLES BARRY born (died 1860). Architect. Houses of Parliament; Harewood; Shrubland Hall, Suffolk; Cliveden, Buckinghamshire

1801 SIR JOSEPH PAXTON born (died 1865). Gardener and Architect. Garden at Chatsworth, Derbyshire. The Crystal Palace and its garden at Sydenham. House and garden at Mentmore, Buckinghamshire

c. 1806 Cliff Garden at Hawkestone, Shropshire, and Quarry Garden at Belsay Castle, Northumberland, begun

1822 *An Encyclopaedia of Gardening*, edited by John Claudius Loudon

1826 *The Gardener's Magazine*, edited by John Claudius Loudon

1836 *The Suburban Gardener and Villa Companion*, by John Claudius Loudon

1838 WILLIAM ROBINSON born (died 1900). Editor of *Gardening Illustrated*. Own garden at Gravetye Manor, Sussex

1842 Garden at Biddulph Grange, Staffordshire, begun by James Bateman
Garden at Scotney Castle, Kent, begun, on advice from William Sawrey Gilpin, by Edward Hussey, on completion of new house

1843 GERTRUDE JEKYLL born (died 1932). Artist. Own garden at Munstead Wood, Surrey. With Sir Edwin Lutyens, gardens at Marsh Court, Surrey; Hestercombe, Somerset; The Deanery, Sonning, Berkshire

1844 Palm House at Kew designed by Decimus Burton

1845 Osborne House acquired by Queen Victoria

1850 *How To Lay Out A Garden*, by Edward Kemp

1854 HAROLD PETO born (died 1933). Garden at Buscot, Berkshire. Own garden at Iford Manor, Wiltshire

1859 *The Town Garden*, by Shirley Hibberd

c. 1860 Rhododendron Garden at Leonardslee, Sussex, begun by Sir Edmund Loder

1863 Garden at Cragside, Northumberland, begun by William George, later 1st Baron, Armstrong

1869 SIR EDWIN LUTYENS born (died 1944). Architect. New Delhi. Gardens at Great Dixter, Sussex; Castle Drogo, Devonshire; Blagdon, Northumberland. Worked with Gertrude Jekyll

1874 Garden at Ascott, Wing, Buckinghamshire, begun by Baron Leopold de Rothschild

1883 *The English Flower Garden*, by William Robinson

1892 V. SACKVILLE-WEST born (died 1962). Author. Wife of Harold Nicolson. Gardening Correspondent of the *Observer*. Own garden at Sissinghurst Castle, Kent

1905 Japanese Garden at Cottered, Cambridgeshire, begun by Herbert Goode

1906 Garden at Hidcote Manor, Gloucestershire, begun by Major Lawrence Johnston. Existing Layout 1913. Alleys of Pleached Hornbeam 1915

1908 *Colour in the Flower Garden*, by Gertrude Jekyll

1910 *The Genus Rosa*, by Ellen Willmott. Artist and Gardener. Own garden at Warley Place, Essex

1912 Garden at Port Lympne, Kent, begun by Sir Philip Sassoon

1918 Garden at Muncaster, Cumbria, re-modelled by Sir John Ramsden

1920 Garden at Compton Acres, Poole, Dorset, begun by Thomas William Simpson
Garden at Sheffield Park, Sussex, extensively planted with shrubs, over existing Brown and Repton landscape, by Arthur G. Soames

1924 Knot Garden at Hampton Court laid out

1925 Garden at Titinhull, Somerset (laid out *c.* 1900) re-planted by Mrs. Reis

1932 Savill Gardens in Windsor Great Park begun by Col. Eric Savill

1934 Parterre Garden at Ditchley Park, Oxfordshire, laid out by Geoffrey Jellicoe

1937 Garden at Bentley's, Sussex, by Christopher Tunnard and Serge Chermayeff.

1939 Long Water at Blagdon, Northumberland, completed by Sir Edwin Lutyens

1947 Garden at The Hunting Lodge, Odiham, Hampshire, begun by John Fowler

1950s Garden at Badminton Cottage, Gloucestershire, by Russell Page for Lady Caroline Somerset
Garden at Haseley Court, Oxfordshire, made by Mrs. Nancy Lancaster

1960 Garden at Moseley Old Hall, West Midlands, re-constructed by Miles Hadfield for The National Trust

1975 Victorian and Elizabethan Gardens at Temple Newsam, Yorkshire, begun by Leeds City Council.

1977 Jubilee Garden on South Bank in London completed by Greater London Council

Sir Joseph Paxton

Gertrude Jekyll

Appendix Two

Places improved by Charles Bridgeman (?–1738)

Compiled from *Parks in England* by Hugh Prince

Amesbury Abbey, Wilts	1730–8	Cassiobury Park, Herts	
Blenheim Palace, Oxon	1709–38	Chiswick House, Middx	?1715–20
Boughton House, Northants	1726–31	Claremont House, Surrey	1729
Bower House, Essex	1729	Down Hall, Essex	1720–7
Carshalton House, Surrey	1719–21	Eastbury Park, Dorset	1725

Hampton Court Palace, Mddx	1726–38	St. James's Park, London	?1738
Houghton Hall, Norfolk	1731	Standlynch, Wilts	1733
Hyde Park, London	1726–38	Stowe, Bucks	1713–38
Kensington Palace, London	1726–38	Wimpole Hall, Cambs	1720–4
King's College, Cambridge	1724	Windsor Castle, Berks	1729–38
Langleys, Essex	1719	Wolterton Hall, Norfolk	1727–38
Marble Hill, Mddx	1724	Wotton House, Bucks	
Richmond, Surrey	1735–8		

Places improved by William Kent (1685–1748)

?Badminton House, Gloucs	c. 1745	?Kew Palace, Surrey	1730
Carlton House, London	1733	?Pains Hill, Surrey	c. 1735
Castle Hill, Devon	1732	?Raynham Hall, Norfolk	c. 1730
Chiswick, Mddx	1719–34	?Richings, Bucks	c. 1720–35
Cirencester (Oakley Wood), Gloucs	c. 1720	Richmond Park, Surrey	1735
		Rousham, Oxon	1738–41
Claremont, Surrey	1719–34	?Shotover, Oxon	c. 1734
?Ditchley Park, Oxon	1726	Stowe, Bucks	c. 1730–48
?Easton Neston, Northants	c. 1730–40	?White Lodge, Richmond, Surrey	1731–5
Euston Hall, Suffolk	1746		
Holkham Hall, Norfolk	1720–34	?Wilton House, Wilts	1732–8
?Houghton Hall, Norfolk	1721–35	? Woburn Farm, Chertsey, Surrey	1735
Kensington Palace, London	c. 1725–44		

Places improved by Lancelot Brown (1715–1783)

Alnwick Castle, Northumbs	c. 1760–5	Brocklesby Park, Lincs	1772
Althorp, Northants	1780	Burghley House, Northants	1756–81
Ampthill Park, Beds	1771	Burton Constable, Yorks	1772–4
Appuldurcombe, Isle of Wight	c. 1778	Burton Pynsent, Soms	1765
Ashburnham Place, Sussex	c. 1767	Cadland, Hants	1775–9
Ashridge, Herts	1759–68	Cardiff Castle, Glams	1777
Audley End, Essex	1763–6	Castle Ashby, Northants	1761–7
Aynhoe Park, Northants	1760–3	Caversham Park, Berks	c. 1776
?Badminton House, Gloucs	c. 1770	Charlecote Park, Warks	1760–6
Basildon Park, Berks	1778	Charlton Park, Wilts	1765–7
Belhus, Essex	1753–61	Chatsworth, Derbys	c. 1761
Benham Park, Berks	1770–5	Chilham Castle, Kent	1777
Berrington Hall, Herefs	1779–81	Chillington Hall, Staffs	c. 1763
Blenheim Palace, Oxon	1765	?Chiswick House, Mddx	c. 1781
Bowood, Wilts	1761–8	Clandon Park, Surrey	1775
Broadlands, Hants	1765	Claremont House, Surrey	1752–72
		Cliveden, Bucks	1777

Combe Abbey, Warks	1770–3	Nuneham Courtenay, Oxon	1778
Compton Verney, Warks	c. 1768	Oakly Park, Salop	1772–5
Compton Wynyates, Warks	c. 1767	Paultons, Hants	1772
Corsham Court, Wilts	1760–80	Petworth, Sussex	1752
Croome Court, Worcs	1751	?Prior Park, Soms	1765
Dodington Park, Gloucs	1764	Ragley Hall, Warks	1758
Euston Hall, Suffolk	1767	Redgrave Hall, Suffolk	1763
?Gibside, Durham	c. 1760–70	Richmond Park, Surrey	1771–3
Grimsthorpe Castle, Lincs	1771	St. John's College, Cambridge	1772–9
Hallingbury Place, Essex	1778	Sandbeck Park, Yorks	1766–74
Hampton Court, Mddx	1765	Sandleford Priory, Berks	1781–3
Hampton House, Mddx	1754–8	Scampston Hall, Yorks	1773
Harewood House, Yorks	1772–82	Sheffield Park, Sussex	1776
?Hartwell House, Bucks	c. 1749	Sherborne Castle, Dorset	1756–79
Heveningham Hall, Suffolk	1781–2	Southill Park, Beds	1777
Holkham Hall, Norfolk	1762	Stansted Park, Sussex	1781–3
Ickworth, Suffolk	1767–76	Stapleford Park, Leics	1775
Kimberley Hall, Norfolk	1762	Stowe, Bucks	1748–51
Kings Weston, Gloucs	1777	Syon House, Mddx	1762–73
Kirtlington Park, Oxon	1751–62	Temple Newsam, Yorks	1765–7
Knowsley, Lancs	1775	Thoresby Hall, Notts	c. 1768
Langley Park, Bucks	1765	Thorndon Hall, Essex	1766–72
Leeds Castle, Kent	1771	Tong Castle, Salop	1765
Longford Castle, Wilts	1776	Trentham Park, Staffs	1764–78
Longleat, Wilts	1757–62	Ugbrooke, Devon	1761
Lowther Castle, Westmorland	1763	Wallington Hall, Northumbs	c. 1766
Luton Hoo, Beds	1764–70	Wardour Castle, Wilts	1780
Mamhead, Devon	1772–9	Warwick Castle, Warks	1748–59
Melton Constable, Norfolk	1764	Weston, Staffs	1763–8
Milton Abbey, Dorset	1763–73	Wilton House, Wilts	1778
Moccas Court, Herefs	1778	Wimbledon Park, Surrey	1755–80
Moor Park, Herts	1759	Wimpole Hall, Cambs	1767–73
Mount Clare, Roehampton, Surrey	1773	Wrest Park, Beds	1758
		Wycombe Abbey, Bucks	1762–8

Places improved by Humphry Repton (1752–1818)

Adlestrop Park, Gloucs	1799–1812	Aston Hall, Ches	c. 1793
Antony House, Cornwall	c. 1794	Attingham Hall, Salop	1798
Ashridge, Herts	1814	Bayham Abbey, Kent	1800
		Betchworth, Surrey	1800

Blaise Castle, Gloucs	1796	Longleat, Wilts	1803
Bickling Hall, Norfolk	c. 1794	Longner Hall, Salop	1804
Bowood, Wilts	c. 1803	Luscombe Castle, Devon	1799
Brighton Pavilion, Sussex	1797, 1806	Magdalen College,	
Brookmans Park, Herts	c. 1794	Oxford	1801
Bristol, The Fort, Soms	c. 1803	Marks Hall, Essex	1789
Bulstrode Park, Bucks	1790	Milton, Northants	1791
Burley-on-the-		Moccas Court, Herefs	c. 1798
Hill, Rutland	1795	Mulgrave Castle, Yorks	1793
Caerhays Castle,		Nacton Hall, Suffolk	c. 1794
Cornwall	c. 1809	Normanton Park,	
Carlton House, London	1803	Rutland	c. 1803
Cassiobury Park, Herts	c. 1801	Northrepps Hall,	
Catton, Norfolk	1788	Norfolk	c. 1792
Cobham Hall, Kent	1790	Oulton, Yorks	1810
Condover Hall, Salop	c. 1803	Panshanger, Herts	1799
Corsham Court, Wilts	1796–1810	?Plas Newydd,	
Courteenhall, Northants	1791	Anglesey	c. 1803
Crewe Hall, Ches	1791	Port Eliot, Cornwall	1792
Culford Hall, Suffolk	c. 1794	Prestwood, Staffs	1790
Donington Hall, Leics	1790	Rendlesham Hall,	
Dulwich Casina, Surrey	1797	Suffolk	c. 1803
Dyrham, Gloucs	1801–3	Rivenhall Place,	
Endsleigh, Devon	1810	Essex	c. 1794
Felbrigg Hall, Norfolk	1807–10	Rudding Park, Yorks	1790
Garnons, Herefs	1791	Rhûg, Merioneth	1793
Gayhurst, Bucks	c. 1793	St. John's Ryde, Isle	
Glemham Hall, Suffolk	c. 1803	of Wight	c. 1798
Great Tew, Oxon	1803	Sarsden House, Oxon	1795
Gunton Hall, Norfolk	1816	Scarisbrick Hall, Lancs	1802
Harewood House, Yorks	1800	Sezincote, Glos	1804–5
Hasells Hall, Beds	1790	Shardeloes, Bucks	before 1796?
Hatchlands, Surrey	1800	Sheffield Park, Sussex	1789
Heathfield Park,		Sheringham Hall,	
Sussex	c. 1803	Norfolk	1812–7
Henham Hall, Suffolk	1791	?Shrubland Park, Suffolk	
Herriard Park, Hants	c. 1794	Stanage Park, Radnor	1803
Hewell Grange, Worcs		Stanmore House, Mddx	
Holkham, Norfolk	1788	Stanstead Hall, Essex	1790
Hurlingham, Mddx	c. 1803	Stoke Edith, Herefs	c. 1794
Kenwood, London	c. 1797	Stoke Poges, Bucks	1792–9
Kidbrooke Park, Sussex	c. 1806	Ston Easton Park, Soms	c. 1794
Langley Park, Kent	1790	Stratton Park, Hants	c. 1803
?Langleys, Essex	c. 1803	Sundridge, Kent	c. 1794
Lathom Hall, Lancs	c. 1795	Taplow Court, Bucks	c. 1803
Livermere Park,		Tatton Park, Ches	1792
Suffolk	1790	Tendring Hall, Suffolk	1790

Thoresby Hall, Notts	1791	West Wycombe Park,	
Tofts Hall, Norfolk	1789	Bucks	c. 1793
Tregothnan, Cornwall	1809	White Lodge, Richmond,	
Trent Park, Mddx		Surrey	1805
Trewarthenick, Cornwall	1793	Whitton Park, Mddx	c. 1803
Tyringham, Bucks	c. 1793	?Wilton House, Wilts	c. 1806
Uppark, Sussex	1805, 1810	Wimpole Hall, Cambs	c. 1798
Wanstead, Essex	c. 1810	Wingerworth Hall, Derby	c. 1791
Warley Place, Essex	1806	Witley Court, Worcs	c. 1816
Welbeck Abbey, Notts	1789	Woburn Abbey, Beds	c. 1800
Wentworth Woodhouse,		Wollaton Hall, Notts	c. 1816
Yorks	1790	Wycombe Abbey, Bucks	c. 1803

Appendix Three

The origin and approximate date of introduction of some plants in common cultivation today, compiled from the Royal Horticultural Society's *Dictionary of Gardening*

Border Plants:

Achillea Europe, North and West Asia, North America. *millefolium* native—*ptarmica* native—*clavenae* Eastern Alps 1656—*filipendulina* Caucasus 1803

Aconitum napellus Europe and Asia, perhaps mediaeval

Althea rosea Orient 1573

Anemone Mostly temperate Northern hemisphere. *pulsatilla* (correctly *Pulsatilla vulgaris*) and *nemorosa* native—*coronaria* Southern Europe and Central Asia 1596—*japonica* China 1844

Antirrhinum majus Europe 16th century

Aquilegia Temperate Northern hemisphere. *vulgaris* native—*canadensis* 1640

Artemisia abrotanum Southern Europe 1548

Aster Temperate Northern hemisphere. *amellus* Italy 1596 (China Aster, *Callistephus chinensis*, China 1731)

Auricula Europe. Descendants of *Primula auricula* European Alps 1596 and *Primula x pubescens*, probably a hybrid of *P. auricula* and *P. rubra* Central Alps, Pyrenees 16th century

Bergenia Temperate Asia. *crassifolia* Siberia 1765 *cordifolia* Siberia 1779

Calendula officinalis Southern Europe 1573

Campanula Temperate Northern hemisphere. *latifolia, glomerata, rotundifolia, persicifolia* native—*pyramidalis* Europe 1596—*Medium* Southern Europe 1597—*lactiflora*

245

Caucasus 1814—*latiloba* Siberia 1842

Cheiranthus cheiri   Europe, now naturalised, perhaps mediaeval

Chrysanthemum   Temperate Northern hemisphere. *parthenium* native—*maximum* Pyrenees (not known)—*uliginosum* Hungary (not known)—*rubellum* (not known) 1929. Florists' chrysanthemums are hybrids, mostly from China and Japan

Colchicum autumnale   native

Convallaria majalis   native

Cosmos   Mexico. *bipinnatus* 1799—*astrosanguineus* 1835

Crinum   Sub-tropics. *bulbispermum* South Africa 1752—*Moorei* Natal 1874, parents of *Crinum x Powellii*

Crocus   Central and Southern Europe, North Africa, Asia Minor to Afghanistan. *aureus* Eastern Europe, before 1597—*byzantinus* Carpathians, before 1629

Cyclamen   Mediterranean, Asia Minor. *neapolitanum* perhaps Roman

Dahlia   Mexico. *coccinea* and *rosea* 1798—*Juarezii* 1864

Delphinium   Europe, Asia, North America, mountains of Africa. *ajacis* Southern Europe, very early—*formosum* Caucasus early 19th century—*Brunonianum* Afghanistan to Western China 1864—*grandiflorum* Siberia, Western North America 19th century—*nudicaule* California 1869

Dianthus   Europe, Mediterranean, Asia, mountains of Africa. *deltoides, Armeria, gratianopolitanus* native—*barbatus* South and East Europe 1573—*Caryophyllus* South and West France 16th century—*plumarius* South East Europe 1629

Digitalis   Europe, North Africa, West Asia. *purpurea* native—*ambigua* Europe 1596—*orientalis* Near East 17th century (?)

Doronicum   Europe, temperate Asia. *Pardalianches, plantagineum* native

Erigeron   Temperate Northern hemisphere. *alpinus* native—*mucronatus* Mexico early 19th century—*speciosus* Western North America 1889

Eryngium   World wide, temperate and sub-tropical regions. *alpinum* Europe 1597–*amethystianum* Europe 1648—*Bourgati* Pyrenees 1731

Euphorbia   World wide. *lathyrus* Europe, perhaps Roman—*Wulfenii, epithymoides* Europe (not known)—*pilosa major* Europe and Northern Asia, probably 19th century

Fritillaria   Northern hemisphere. *meleagris* native—*imperialis* Western Himalaya before 1590

Gaillardia   North America. *aristata* Western States 1812

Geranium   All temperate regions. *pratense, sanguineum, sylvaticum* native—*macrorrhizum* Southern Europe 1576—*Wallichianum* Himalaya 1820—*psilostemon* Armenia 19th century. Scarlet Geraniums are Pelargoniums

Geum   Temperate regions. *rivale* native—*Chiloense* Chile 1826

Gladiolus   Europe, Mediterranean, tropical and South Africa. *illyricus* native—*byzantinus* Corsica eastwards 1629—*blandus* South Africa 1774—*cardinalis* South Africa 1789. Hybrids from these *c.*1860 onwards.

Glaucium flavum   native

Godetia   North America. *amoena* Western States 1818—*grandiflora* California 1867

Gypsophila   Eastern Mediterranean, Asia. *paniculata* Eastern Europe, Siberia 1759

Helianthus   North America, Chile, Peru. *annuus* Peru 1596—*tuberosus* Canada, Arkansas, Georgia 1617—*lactiflorus* mid U.S. 1810—*decapetalus* Canada late 18th century (?) *debilis* Southern States 1883

Heliotropium   World wide tropics. *peruvianum* Peru 1757—*corymbosum* Peru 1808

Helleborus Southern Europe, Western Asia, Britain. *foetidus, viridis* native—*niger* Central and Southern Europe, Western Asia probably mediaeval—*orientalis* Greece, Asia Minor 1829—*corsicus* Corsica, Sardinia, Balearic Isles 19th century

Hemerocallis Temperate Eastern Asia. *flava* China (?) 1570—*fulva* (not know) 1576

Heuchera North America. *americana* 1656—*micrantha* British Columbia to California 1827—*sanguinea* North Mexico, Arizona 1882

Hosta Eastern Asia. *ventricosa* Eastern Asia 1790—others from Japan from 1829

Hyacinthus Mediterranean, Asia Minor. *orientalis* Italy to Mesopotamia perhaps mediaeval, possibly Roman—*romanus* Southern France, North Africa 1596—*amethystianus* Pyrenees 1759

Hypericum Northern hemisphere. *Androsaemum* native—*calycinum* Asia Minor 1676

Iberis Europe, Western Asia. *amara* native—*sempervirens* Southern Europe 1731

Impatiens Mountains of Asia and Africa. *balsimina* India, Malaya, China 1596

Iris Entire Northern hemisphere. *foetidissima, pseudo-acorus* native—*germanica, illyrica* (*cengialti*) Europe probably mediaeval—*Xiphium* Southern France to Portugal 1596

Kentranthus Europe, Mediterranean. *ruber* perhaps Roman, naturalised

Kniphofia South and East Africa, Madagascar. *uvaria* South Africa 1707—others 19th century

Lavandula Mediterranean, Canary Isles, India. *spica* Mediterranean 1568

Lavatera Europe. *olbia rosea* Southern France 1570

Leucojum autumnale Portugal, Morocco 1629

Lilium Temperate Northern hemisphere. *candidum* Mediterranean mediaeval—*martagon* Europe, Asia 1596—*pyrenaicum* Pyrenees 1596—*chalcedonicum* Greece 1600—*canadense* North America 1620—*superbum* Eastern States 1738—*monadelphum* Caucasus 1804—*tigrinum* China, Korea, Japan 1804—*speciosum* Japan 1832—*Brownii* China 1835—*auratum* Japan 1862—*longiflorum* Formosa 1862—*regale* China 1903

Linaria Northern hemisphere, South America. *purpurea* Southern Europe 1648

Linum World wide, temperate regions. *perenne* native—*narbonense* Southern Europe 1759—*flavum* Germany to Russia 1793—*monogynum* New Zealand 1822

Lupinus North and South America, Mediterranean. *hirsutus* Southern Europe, probably 16th century—*perennis* Eastern States 1658—*arboreus* California 1793—*polyphyllus* Western States 1826

Malva Southern Europe, North Africa, temperate Asia. *moschata* native—*alcea* Europe 1797—*alcea fastigiata* Italy 1820

Meconopsis Western Europe, North India, Upper Burma, Western China. *cambrica* native—most others 20th century

Matthiola South and West Europe, Western Asia. *sinuata* native—*incana* Southern Europe, early 16th century (?). Garden stocks from these.

Muscari Black Sea, Mediterranean. *comosum* Europe 1596—*botyroides* Europe 1896

Myosotis Europe and Australia. *alpestris, scorpioides, sylvatica* native

Narcissus Europe, North Africa, Western Asia. *obvallaris, pseudonarcissus* native—*aureus* Southern France before 1600—*bulbocodium* Iberia, North Africa 1629

Nemesia South Africa. *linearis* 1822—*strumosa* 1892

Nepeta Temperate Northern hemisphere. *Cataria, hederacea* native—*Mussinii* Caucasus, Persia 19th century

Nicotiana Tropical America. *rustica, Tabacum* about 1580—*alata* (*affinis*) Brazil 19th century—*sylvestris* Argentina 1898

Nigella   Mediterranean, Western Asia. *damascena* Mediterranean 1570—*hispanica* Spain, Southern France 1629

Paeonia   Europe, temperate Asia, North-west America, China. *officinalis* France to Albania 1548—*humilis* Southern France 1633—*lactiflora* Siberia, Mongolia 1784—*suffruticosa* China, Tibet, Bhutan 1787

Papaver   Asia, North Africa, Europe. *Rhoeas* probably Asia, Celtic—*somniferum* Far East, Celtic—*orientale* Armenia 1714—*nudicaule* Iceland 1759

Petunia   South America. *intergrifolia* Argentina 1831—*nyctaginiflora* Brazil 1823

Phlox   North America. *paniculata* Eastern States 1732—*Drummondii* Texas, New Mexico 1835

Polyanthus   Descendants of a natural cross between *Primula acaulis* and *Primula veris* known as the Oxlip. Coloured forms appeared in the seventeenth century.

Polygonatum   Northern hemisphere. *multiflorum, officinale* native

Primula   Principally temperate Northern hemisphere. *acaulis, elatior, veris* native—*auricula* Alps 1596—*auriculata* Caucasus 1794—*japonica* 1874—Himalayan species mostly 20th century

Pulmonaria   Europe. *longifolia* native—*officinalis* probably mediaeval

Ranunculus   Mostly temperate Northern hemisphere. *asiaticus* Asia Minor 1596—*aconitifolius* Europe 1596

Rosa   Asia, America, Europe, North West Africa. *canina, eglanteria* native—*arvensis, spinossissima* native (?)—*alba* (not known) probably mediaeval—*gallica* France mediaeval—*damascena* Asia Minor 1573—*centifolia* Caucasus 1596—*foetida* Caspian before 1600—*chinensis* China 1768—*odorata* China 1810—*rugosa* Japan, Korea, China 1845

Rosmarinus   Southern Europe, Asia Minor. *officinalis* mediaeval

Rudbeckia   North America. *laciniata* 1640—*triloba* 1699—*hirta* 1714

Ruta graveolens   Southern Europe 1562

Salvia   World wide, temperate and sub-tropical. *pratensis* native—*sclarea* Mediterranean probably 16th century—*officinalis* Southern Europe 1597—*splendens* Brazil 1822

Santolina   Mediterranean. *Chamaecyparissus* 1596—*virens* 1727—*pinnata* 1791—*neapolitana* (not known)

Saxifraga   Europe, North America. *umbrosa* native

Scabiosa   Mediterranean, Western Asia. *Columbaria, Succisa* native—*atropurpurea* South West Europe 1629—*caucasica* Caucasus 1803

Scilla   Europe, temperate Asia and Africa. *nonscripta* native—*hispanica* Iberia 1683—*sibirica* Siberia 1796

Sidalcea   Western North America. *malvaeflora* California 1838

Stachys   Temperate Northern hemisphere. *officinalis* native—*lanata* Caucasus to Persia 1782—*macrantha* Caucasus 1800

Tagetes   Tropical America. *patula* Mexico 1573—*erecta* Mexico 17th century

Trollius   Temperate Northern hemisphere. *europeaus* native—*asiaticus* Siberia, Turkestan before 1823—*chinensis* Northern China 1912

Tropaeolum   South America. *minus* 1585—*majus* 17th century

Tulipa   Mediterranean, Western Asia. *sylvestris* native—*Gesneriana* Turkey from 1554 (origin uncertain)

Verbascum   Mediterranean, Western and Central Asia. *blattaria, nigra* native—*phlomoides* Caucasus 1739—*phoeniceum* Southern Europe, Western Asia 1796

Viola   World wide, temperate zones. *lutea, odorata, riviniana, tricolor* native—*cornuta* Pyrenees 1796—*altaica* Caspian 1805. Garden pansies hybrids, frequently of these.

Zinnia elegans   Mexico 1796

Shrubs, Climbers, some Garden Trees:

Acer   Temperate Northern hemisphere. *negundo* North America 1688—*palmatum* Japan 1820—*japonicum* Japan 1864

Arbutus unedo   Southern Europe, Ireland, Asia Minor. Very early

Aucuba japonica   Japan 1783

Berberis   Principally Himalayas, China, Japan. 19th and 20th centuries

Buddleia   Temperate America, South Africa, Asia. *globosa* Chile, Peru 1774—*Davidii* China 1896—*alternifolia* China 1915

Camellia   Tropical and sub-tropical Asia. *japonica* Korea 1739

Catalpa   Eastern Asia, North and South America. *bignonoides* Eastern States 1726—*Fargesii* China 1900

Ceanothus   North America. *Americanus* 1713—mostly 19th century

Cercis   Europe, North America, China. *siliquastrum* Southern Europe 16th century

Chaenomeles   Eastern Asia. *lagenaria* Japan 1796—*japonica* 1869

Clematis   Temperate regions of both hemispheres. *vitalba* native—*montana* Himalayas 1831—Jackmanii Hybrids from about 1870—*Armandii* China 1900

Choisya ternata   Mexico 1825

Colutea   South Europe to Himalayas. *arborescens* 16th century—*orientalis* Orient 1710

Cornus   Temperate Northern hemisphere. *sanguinea* native—*mas* Europe perhaps mediaeval—*alba* Siberia 1741

Cotoneaster   Mostly Himalayas, Western and Central China. *tomentosa* 1759—others 19th and 20th centuries

Daphne   Europe, Himalayas, China. *laureola, mezereum* native—*pontica* Caucasus 1752—*odora* China, Japan 1771

Deutzia   Himalayas, China, Japan. 19th and 20th centuries

Elaeagnus   Temperate Northern hemisphere. *angustifolia* Europe, Western Asia 16th century—*pungens* Japan 1830

Escallonia   South America, principally Chile. From 1848

Euonymus   Temperate regions, both hemispheres. *europaeus* native—*japonicus* 1804

Fatsia japonica   Japan 1838

Forsythia   Eastern Asia, South East Europe. *viridissima* Eastern China 1844—*suspensa* Eastern China 1850

Fuchsia   South America, New Zealand. *magellanica* Peru, Chile 1823

Garry elliptica   Oregon 1828

Griselinia littoralis   New Zealand 1872

Hamamelis   North America, Eastern Asia. *virginiana* Eastern States 1736—*mollis* China 1879

Hydrangea   North and South America, Eastern Asia. *arborescens* Northern States 1736—*macrophylla* Japan 1790—*quercifolia* South Eastern States 1803—*paniculata* China, Japan 1861—*Sargentiana* China 1908

Jasminum   World wide. *humile*—South East Europe 1656—*nudiflorum* China 1844

Laburnum   Southern Europe, Western Asia. *anagyroides*—Southern Europe 1560—
alpinum Southern Europe 1596

Laurus nobilis   Southern Europe 1562

Ligustrum ovalifolium   Japan 1842

Lonicera   Northern hemisphere. *periclymenum* native—*caprifolium* Europe, perhaps 16th
century—*sempervirens* United States 1656—*japonica* Japan, Korea, China 1806—*nitida*
China 1908

Magnolia   North and Central America, Himalayas, Eastern Asia. *virginiana* Virginia
1688—*grandiflora* South Eastern States 1737—*denudata* China 1789—*liliflora* China
1790 (parents of Soulangeana)

Mahonia   Northern Asia, Central America. 19th and 20th centuries.

Malus   Northern hemisphere. *pumila* native—*baccata* Eastern Asia, Northern China
1784—*floribunda* Japan 1862

Philadelphus   North America, South Europe, Asia. *coronarius* Southern Europe, Asia
Minor 1596—others mostly 19th century

Phlomis fruticosa   Mediterranean 1596

Potentilla fruticosa   native

Prunus   Northern hemisphere, South America. *avium* native—*cerasifera* Western Asia,
Caucasus perhaps pre-Roman—*laurocerasus* Eastern Europe, Asia Minor 1629—
lusitanica Spain, Portugal 1648—*serrulata* China, Japan 1822—*subhirtella* Japan 1895—
incisa Japan 1913

Pyracantha   Europe, temperate Asia. *coccinea* Southern Europe, Asia Minor 1629—
atalantoides China 1907—*Rogersiana* China 1911

Pyrus   Mediterranean, North East Asia. *communis* perhaps pre-Roman—*salicifolia*
Europe, Asia Minor 1870

Rhododendron   Caucasus, Himalayas, China ('Azaleas' from North America, Japan).
maximum North America 1736—*ponticum* Spain, Portugal, Asia Minor 1763—*luteum*
Eastern Europe, Asia Minor 1793—*caucasicum* Caucasus 1803—*catawbiense* North
America 1809—*arboreum* Himalayas 1815—*Augustinii* China 1901

Rhus   Temperate regions both hemispheres. *typhina*—Eastern United States 1629—
cotinus Eastern Europe, Caucasus 1656—*copallina* North America 1688

Ribes   Northern hemisphere, Patagonia. *sanguineum* Western United States 1826

Senecio   World wide. *laxifolius* New Zealand 19th century

Skimmia japonica   China, Japan 1838

Sorbus   Europe, North America, Northern Asia. *aria, aucuparia, torminalis* native—
domestica Europe, very early

Symphoricarpos   United States, China. *rivularis* Northern States 1817

Syringa   North Eastern Asia, Eastern Europe. *vulgaris* Eastern Europe 16th century—
persica Persia 1640

Viburnum   Principally temperate Northern hemisphere. *lantana, opulus* native—*tinus*
South Eastern Europe 1560—*tomentosum* China, Japan 1865

Weigela (now Diervilla)   North America, Eastern Asia. *lonicera* Eastern States 1734—
others mostly 19th century

Wisteria   North America, China, Japan. *frutescens* North America 1724–*sinensis* China
1816—*floribunda* Japan 1830

Notes to the Colour Plates

The oxlip is a natural cross between the primrose and the cowslip, cestor of the modern Polyanthus.

One of our two irises. The other is the Gladwyn, *Iris foetidissima*. *ora Londinensis* was first published in 1777. (The John Innes stitute)

The blackberry is native. Its leaves, pressed to the chest, were ought to cure heartburn.

Henbane, a native, long grown in gardens for its narcotic operties.

Agrimony, a native, possibly the Hemp Agrimony. Both had very ugh stalks which could be twisted into ropes.

Alexanders, *Smyrnium olusatrum*. Native to Southern Europe. as a flavour like very strong celery. Grown in kitchen gardens into e 19th century. Now wild, especially in Norfolk.

The Bury Herbal was written in Anglo-Saxon. (Bodley 130)

Reconstructed Garden at Pompeii. (Photo: Gerald Sunderland)

The Romance of the Rose is a manuscript now in the British brary. (Harley 4425)

The 'fleur de lys' of heraldry, *Iris germanica*.

The 'gillyflower' is constantly referred to by poets and garden riters. It was a hybrid dianthus, possibly including the carnation. order pinks' or 'border carnations' would be as close as we could me today.

The Herbal and Bestiary ABC is thought to have been made 'for e instruction and amusement of the young'. The captions were in glish, but the artist is thought to have been Flemish. Water rking on original. (Bodleian Library, Ashmole 1504)

The yellow violet, *Viola lutea*, ancestor of our garden pansies.

The 'French' marigold, *Tagetes patula*, native to Mexico. *Nigella* native to the Mediterranean.

Possibly *Narcissus calcicola*.

Ipomœa Jalapa was introduced from the South-Eastern United ates in 1633. The gladiolus is probably *byzantinus*.

Alexander Marshall, first of the English flower painters, died in lham in 1682. (The British Museum)

Cheveley Park. The flower garden and the vegetable garden parated by the house. (Photo: Gerald Sunderland)

Llanerch. It was this kind of garden that John Rea wrote about. ale Center for British Art, Paul Mellon Collection. Photo: Gerald underland)

Pierrepont House, Nottingham. Gardens not unlike this were sited by Celia Fiennes, particularly at Epsom. (Unknown Dutch inter, Yale Center for British Art, Paul Mellon Collection. Photo: erald Sunderland)

Dunham Massey. The kind of garden about which John orlidge wrote. The mount and avenues date from this time, 1696. he National Trust. Photo: Gerald Sunderland)

-8 Hampton Court, Herefordshire. The canal, with its single row trees, is outside the wall, and the formal tree planting continues to the countryside. The gazebo has replaced the mount as a point of ntage. (Yale Center for British Art, Paul Mellon Collection)

-30 The house at Stoke Edith was begun about 1690 and these ngings probably represent the original garden. They were made, er a great many years, by the ladies of the house. (Photo: *Country fe*)

-4 The manor house, at Dixton, still exists. The garden, at this

time, was small and square. The second painting is a superb representation of the 'unimproved' landscape. Morris dancers and haymakers in the fields. (Cheltenham Museum and Art Gallery, Photo: Gerald Sunderland)

35 The Duchess of Beaufort's Book is a collection of paintings by 'Mr. Kychious' and Daniel Frankcom 'a servant of My Lady Duchess', of exotic or unusual flowers which bloomed at Badminton between 1703 and 1705.

36 The nerine is native to South Africa. The ship carrying some of the bulbs was wrecked off the coast of Guernsey. Washed ashore, the bulbs grew and the plant became known in England as the Guernsey Lily.

37 Simply called 'A geranium from the Cape'.

38 'Rais'd of a seed 1692 has bore fruit till 1700 it is 12 foot high & had been much taller if the stove had been higher'. The guava is native to sub-tropical America.

39 '*Alcea Maxima*', now called *Hibiscus Abelmoschus*, grown in India for its flowers and musk-scented seeds. (The Duke and Duchess of Beaufort)

40–4 Hartwell House, Buckinghamshire. Probably laid out in the 1690s, these paintings show the garden in 1738. The HaHa would have been new then, and it appears to have had a hedge along it. The trees now make a 'wilderness' outside the formal garden and the buildings in it, by James Gibbs, would also be new—possibly one reason for having this series of paintings made. (Buckinghamshire County Museum. Photos: Gerald Sunderland)

45 Native to Brazil, the pineapple probably arrived in England via Portugal, perhaps with Catherine of Braganza, Queen of Charles II. (RHS)

46 Probably *Citrus nobilis*. (Unknown Artist. RHS)

47 Thomas Robins the Younger led a sad life. He left behind him a superb series of paintings (similar to this one), of flowers from life. The lily is *Lilium pyrenaicum* and the Pyrenean Houndstongue probably *Cynoglossum cherifolium*. (The Earl and Countess of Scarbrough)

48 *Inula helenium*. Native.

49 *Helianthus tuberosus*. North America 1617.

50 *Aconitum napellus*. Europe very early.

51 *Mirabilis Jalapa*. Peru 1596.

From *Plantes de Toornfort*, paintings by M. Billerer of Besançon. (The Earl and Countess of Scarbrough)

52 Dunham Massey. The mount has been retained (and exists today), the tree planting is extensive and almost entirely formal and a huge kitchen garden has been made on the other side of the high road. (The National Trust. Photo: Gerald Sunderland).

53–4 Claremont, Surrey. Bridgeman's amphitheatre retained by Kent, who took over the landscaping in 1729. The building on the island is by him. (Private collection. Photos: John Bethell)

55 Claude Gelée le Lorrain, also called Claude Lorrain, came from Lorraine. (Photo: The National Trust)

56 Jan Franz van Bloemen (1662–1749), from Anvers, worked in Italy under the name of l'Orizonte. He followed in the tradition of Claude Lorrain and it is likely that Kent brought back this painting for Lord Leicester. Lord Cobham also had two at Stowe. (Holkham Hall, Norfolk. Photo: Gerald Sunderland)

57–9 Chiswick House. A 'patte d'oie' of pleached alleys, possibly by

Bridgeman, who started the landscaping in 1718 for Lord Burlington. The 'amphitheatre', also possibly by Bridgeman, preserved by Kent, here contains the Rotunda, designed by Lord Burlington. The Serpentine River, Oval Pond, River Pavilion and Stone Bridge by Charles Bridgeman. The building on the right, in the third painting, could have been designed by Kent, who certainly designed the grotto at the head of the main canal. (Chatsworth. Photo: Gerald Sunderland)

60 Stowe: The lakeside pavilions by Vanbrugh, about 1720.

61 Gothic Temple by James Gibbs, about 1740.

62 Temple of Ancient Virtue, by William Kent, about 1735.

63 Rotunda by Vanbrugh, about 1720.

64 Temple of British Worthies, by Kent, 1733.

65 Temple of Concord and Victory, by Kent, about 1748.

66 The Palladian Bridge, possibly by James Gibbs, about 1728. (Photos: John Bethell)

67–74 These watercolours show the garden as it was originally intended to be. (The British Museum)

75 Badminton. View from the house towards Worcester Lodge, with other Kent buildings in the park. (The Duke of Beaufort. Photo: Gerald Sunderland)

76 The dotted lines show that there were certain specified viewpoints. (The Art Academy, Stockholm)

81 Detail of a much larger painting. (Cheltenham Museum and Art Gallery. Photo: Gerald Sunderland)

82 (Photo: *Country Life*)

83 Woodside house, Berkshire. The Orangery. (The Basilisk Press)

84 Woodside House, Berkshire. The Chinese House. Nothing remains of this house, or its garden. (The Basilisk Press)

85 (Photo: *Country Life*)

86 Blenheim Palace, Oxfordshire. The lake created by Brown in 1763 partly submerged Vanbrugh's bridge. (Photo: John Bethell)

87 Petworth House, Sussex. View of the park, showing clumps of trees planted by Capability Brown. (The National Trust)

88 Now *Campsis radicans*. Watercolour M.M. 1783 (RHS)

89 Probably *Paeonia peregrina*. Watercolour M.S. 1787. (RHS)

90 *Tropaeolum minus*. Watercolour M.S. 1787 (RHS)

91 Probably *Clematis alpina*. Watercolour M.M. 1789.

92 West Wycombe Park, Buckinghamshire. The painting shows the Music Temple by Nicholas Revett. The park was originally landscaped by Thomas Cook in 1775 and then 'trimmed' by Humphry Repton from 1800. (Photo: *Country Life*)

93–4 'Before' and 'After' at Garnons, Herefordshire, from Repton's Red Book. (Sir John Cotterell. Photo: Gerald Sunderland)

95 Brighton Pavilion, the West Corridor. (Photo: The Bodleian Library)

96 Brighton Pavilion. View from the Private Apartments, showing the flower beds with hooped edges to look like baskets of flowers. (The Bodleian Library)

97 Sezincote, Gloucestershire. 'Indian' house by Samuel Pepys Cockerell, 1805. The curved conservatory joins the house to the octagonal greenhouse. (Mrs David Peake. Photo: Gerald Sunderland)

98 Sezincote. Rock Garden, with Thomas Daniell's 'Indian' bridge in the background, about 1805. (Mrs. David Peake. Photo: Gerald Sunderland)

99 The Pine Strawberry. A cross between a Chilean strawberry and one from Virginia. Ancestor of our modern strawberries. (RHS)

100 The Downton Strawberry. Little is known of it, but presumably it occurred on the estate of Richard Payne Knight (RHS)

101–6 From Regne Vegetal 1831. (RHS)

107 Battlesden Park, Bedfordshire. Painted on completion of the garden for its owner, Gregory Page-Turner. Paxton was gardener boy here. (Page-Turner Collection)

108 Holkham. (Library of Holkham Hall, Norfolk. Photo: Gerald Sunderland)

109–112 Paintings commissioned by an official of the East India Company working in China, and sent home to the Horticultural Society. (RHS)

110 Mrs. Withers became Flower Painter to Queen Adelaide 1830. (RHS)

111 From Robert Sweet's 'Geraniums', 1838. (The Earl and Countess of Scarbrough)

113 From Virginia, 1626.

114 Now *Lychnis coronata*. China and Japan, 1774.

115 Perhaps *Petunia integrifolia*, Argentina 1831.

116 Gloxinias were developed from *Sinningia speciosa*, a native of Brazil.

Paxton's *Magazine of Botany and Register of Flowering Plants* was published between 1834 and 1849. (The John Innes Institute)

121–125 The Hybrid Perpetual Rose was a development of the Bourbon Rose and a stage towards the Hybrid Tea. Of those shown here, only Baroness Rothschild, as she is now called, is still in cultivation. (The John Innes Institute)

130 (Photo: *Country Life*)

131 (Photo: W. J. Bartlett)

132 (Photo: John Bethell)

133 Nyman's, Sussex. Borders in the Walled Garden typical of many planted in the 1920s and 1930s. Colonel Messel also produced a number of notable varieties of garden plant. (Photo: John Bethell)

134–5 Port Lympne, Kent. The Grand Staircase started about 1918 by Philip Tilden and the magnificent double borders, photographed in the 1930s. (Photo: *Country Life*)

136 A glade of azaleas at the Royal Horticultural Society's Garden at Wisley in Surrey. (Photo: *Country Life*)

137 Compton Acres, Poole, Dorset. 'The Japanese Garden', a recent photograph. (Photo: *Country Life*)

138 The first garden gnome, about 1840, now preserved at Lamport Hall, Northamptonshire. The spade is new. (Photo: Mervyn Pickwoad)

Index